There's GOT to be an easier way to run a business

How to have a successful company...and a life!

BILL MARVIN

Hospitality Masters Press
PO Box 280 • Gig Harbor, WA 98335

This publication is intended to provide accurate and authoritative information in regard to the subject matter covered. It is sold with the understanding that the publisher is not engaged in rendering legal, accounting or other professional services. If legal advice or other expert assistance is required, the services of a competent professional person should be sought.

Artwork by Kevin Cordtz, Cordtz Studios, Colorado Springs, CO
ClickArt by T/Maker
Photo Page 163 – Copyright © Stegner Portraits, Colorado Springs, CO

Library of Congress Catalog Card Number: 98-96922

ISBN 0-9656262-6-1

ATTENTION ASSOCIATIONS AND MULTI-UNIT OPERATORS:
Quantity discounts are available on bulk purchases of this book for premiums, sales promotions, educational purposes or fund raising. Custom imprinting or book excerpts can also be created to fit specific needs.

For more information, please contact our Special Sales Department Hospitality Masters Press, PO Box 280, Gig Harbor, WA 98335
(800) 767-1055, e-mail: masters@harbornet.com, Fax: (888) 767-1055
Outside the US and Canada, phone (253) 858-9255, Fax: (253) 851-6887.

There's GOT to Be an Easier Way to Run a Business
How to Have a Successful Company . . . and a Life!

CONTENTS

Part 1
INTRODUCTION

Part 2
OUT OF THE WEEDS

Part 3
A FRESH LOOK AT MANAGEMENT

Part 4
YEAH, BUT . . .

Part 5
WHERE TO FROM HERE?

APPENDIX

Part 1

Introduction

1
Help wanted

If you ran an honest ad for your job, would it look anything like this?

MANAGER WANTED

Must be willing to: sell soul to the company, work 70-80 hours a week for little more than minimum wage, miss children's growing up, lose marriage, start drinking too much, live with stress and die of a coronary at age 53.

Do you think your phone would be ringing off the hook with eager applicants? Of course not . . . and unless this is your idea of a good time, you don't have to put up with this sort of life, either. Easy to say, but what else can you do?

I should point out going into this book that my own background is in the restaurant business. For that reason, the personal examples I give throughout this book will necessarily be from that industry . . . although I think you will find similar examples in your own experience.

Foodservice is a labor-intensive, service-oriented industry that certainly has a reputation for demanding incredibly long hours from its managers. The management model I learned was definitely one of 80+ hour weeks. I graduated from one of the country's premier hospitality degree programs, yet even in school – as in every foodservice job I held – I was taught that this is a killer business where you need to work 18 hours a day, eight days a week. I was told if I was not willing to make that kind of time commitment, I should pursue another line of work.

I never questioned it. I suspect most businesses have a similar myth passed down from one manager to the next. You may have bought into an idea like this, too.

The cost of misunderstanding
The cost we pay for this lack of understanding is staggering. It is measured in lower profits, reduced productivity, burnout, turnover, broken marriages, substance abuse and an impossible level of stress.

The sad truth is that a majority of the problems most managers deal with day after days are not inherent problems of their industry but rather very predictable symptoms of their level of understanding and their idea of what constitutes effective management.

Even as I was working myself to death (120 hours a week in one job!), I couldn't help but feel there just *had* to be an easier way to do what I was doing. I am definitely a hard worker but I am not a masochist, so I started looking for other approaches that might be more effective.

A new model
Perhaps because I was actively looking for a better way, I crossed paths with some folks who were doing breakthrough work in understanding how individuals and organizations really function.

They helped me understand what I was doing in a different way and when I saw a bigger picture, I was suddenly off the old management merry-go-round. The human part of my work became effortless and the difference in my effectiveness was earthshaking!

I know it is easy to think, "In your dreams. It just isn't that easy."

Remember Columbus

If you feel that way, let me remind you that in 1491, the world was flat! Everybody knew the world was flat – it was a fact of life, yet just a year later, it was impossible to hold that view. So that little voice in your head that says, "There's GOT to be an easier way to do this," is right. Once your understanding shifts, your life, professionally and personally, will change forever.

A blinding flash of the obvious

You already have the answers but you just don't see them yet because they are not where you're used to looking. The shift comes when you recognize simple, common sense truths that have been right in front of you all along but which, because of the way you were trained to think, you never fully understood before.

This book will examine the principles that can help you make this shift for yourself . . . if you want to . . . so buckle up and let's get started!

5

2
How to read this book

The shift to a new frame of reference is an inside-out learning process and unfortunately, our education system doesn't teach us much about how to do that.

Outside-in learning
Our model of education is outside-in. It is based on "stuff." (I'm the teacher and I know the stuff. You're a dummy because you don't know the stuff. So I'll tell you about the stuff, you write it all down and then we have a quiz. If you can spit back enough stuff, you will get a good grade and we'll call you educated!)

I don't mean to knock the "stuff" – it is better to know it than to not know it. Knowledge is more powerful than ignorance. But did you ever have a course you took – maybe even one you got a good grade in – that you can't remember a thing about anymore?

The trouble with knowledge is that you only have it as long as you remember it. The shift that will change your personal and professional life is not about more information or finding new tools for your tool belt. It will come from a different understanding . . . and understanding is more powerful than knowledge.

Inside-out learning
When you learn from the inside out, you reach your own insights rather than adopt someone else's views.

For example, I could describe – perhaps eloquently – the view from my deck. I could talk about Puget Sound, Vashon Island, the ferries, the trees and so forth. Perhaps I could even do it well enough that you would start to have a sense of what it must be like. However, you would find it difficult to describe the view to another person with any degree of certainty because you would only have my words to go on.

But if you came to the house and stood on the deck, you would know as much about the view as I do. You would have your own images and could convey your sense of the view as well (or maybe even better) than I might. We would both be on an equal footing as regards the view.

Personally, I would rather get better at giving you directions to the house than get better at describing the view. This is what inside-out learning is like. Here are a few suggestions on how to facilitate this inside-out process of self-learning using this book:

Avoid judgment
Judgment is when you take new information, bounce it off old information and say, "I like this, I do not like that. I agree or I do not agree. Oh, that's what Covey meant when he said . . ." All this will do is keep you stuck in old thinking. It will not help you grow.

7

Read lightly

You have to read a bit differently, too. Typically we read for content, to memorize the key points of the text in preparation for "the quiz." That will not help you. You need to read lightly. Try to get the gist of what I am suggesting, to grasp the spirit behind the message. Try to see the view rather than memorize its description.

Be curious

Roll these ideas around in your brain a little bit. Reflect on how they might be applied. Look for possibilities. Don't try to "make sense" of anything you read, just sit with it awhile and see if it starts to fit. In fact, it is OK to feel in limbo – to not "get it." Getting comfortable in the unknown is the expressway to creative insight.

Validate from experience

Perhaps the strongest idea is to reflect on your personal experience of dealing with people and see if in fact these principles are not directly applicable.

One final suggestion

Human beings seem to like complex constructions. Elaborate theories can be wonderful "mind candy" but you can easily get too clever for your own good. Resist the urge to make these principles complicated. If they are elusive, it is only because of their simplicity and common sense.

The first time through, the ideas in this book may strike you as things you already know. But if you are willing to keep your mind open and re-read the book four or five times, I guarantee you will be struck by exciting insights you missed completely in the first few passes – and that will make all the difference! Trust me on this.

3
Of coaches and cops

No matter what the specific symptoms, people are the common denominators of all business problems. People cause all the problems and people ultimately have to be part of any lasting solutions.

We all say ours is a "people business," but who ever really taught us about people? I suspect most folks became supervisors by decree: "You've been here the longest (you have a degree, your family owns the place, or whatever) so you are the new supervisor. Go out there and supervise."

In truth, few (if any) managers get any real training in what makes people tick. The closest I ever came in my formative years was a psychology course in high school. I learned about paranoid schizophrenics and manic-depressives, but nothing about normal people!

Even my college management courses were closer to advanced manipulation than anything else! Without any deeper understanding to fall back on, we learn to manage by following the model set by our previous managers (most of whom would be in jail if they tried to operate today like they operated then!)

The cop mentality
Most of us were likely mentored by managers who grew up with a cop mentality. "Find things that are wrong and fix them" usually was (and typically still is)

the order of the day for management. This model of supervision is closer to law enforcement than it is to enlightened leadership, but that was what they taught us because that was all they knew.

Cops look for problems and see others as crooks who have to be kept under control at all times. A cop believes that you can compel your staff to deliver quality service and that you can motivate them effectively with fear.

The idea that "the floggings will continue until morale improves" makes sense to a cop. Following the cop model, many people try to force their staff to perform and expect this approach to work.

There is no question that you can get results this way . . . but at what price? One business owner I worked with said, "By any standard, we have been successful. We have been profitable since the day we opened and we are the leaders in the markets we serve. But the price we've paid has been staggering. Our wake is littered with bodies. Surely there has to be an easier way to get the results we want!"

There was a time when we could get away with it, but the cop mentality is seldom effective in the long run because it is an external force and does not properly consider the human factors.

10

The cop model creates organizations that don't work – an unfortunate circumstance that many ascribe to the poor quality of today's workers rather than to the inherent unworkability of the model. However, if you thrive on stress and want to spend the rest of your life looking for the dark side of things, the cop style will certainly give you that result!

The coaching mentality

In the age of service (and we *are* in the age of service if you didn't notice), a more appropriate management style is coaching.

Coaches look for strengths. Coaches see what talent they have to work with and devise a game plan to win with the skills available on the team. Coaches realize that the talent resides in the players and if the players do not develop to *their* full potential, the team will never reach *its* full potential.

Coaches know that motivation is found internally not externally. The best coaches do not try to force people to do anything they do not want to do or are incapable of doing. Like farmers, coaches realize that while contented cows may not necessarily give more milk, they don't kick the bucket over as often and are a lot easier to live with!

Donald I. Smith, former football coach, hospitality industry leader and Professor at Washington State University has always taught that the coach makes the difference. Here are some of his ideas on coaches and coaching that are worth considering:

"Great coaches are first noticed by their uncanny ability to produce championship teams. However, to be called 'coach,' a leader must be measured by more than balance sheets, battles won or lifetime win-loss records.

Great coaches have one more gift. They change the lives of those they touch. I suggest that great coaches can be measured by the number of success stories they leave in their wake. For once they give their players a taste of sweet success, they will have more. They leave behind a legacy of winning which becomes a lifetime habit. The players ultimately become champions of the coach's values, beliefs and passions for the rest of their lives."

When you start to see yourself as a coach, the job changes. The way you measure personal success shifts away from the number of problems you have identified and solved and moves in the direction of tracking the number of wins your staff is enjoying.

To improve your coaching skills, get good at asking questions. Great coaches ask insightful, probing questions that cause their players to think.

It is hard to get yourself in trouble if you are either asking or answering questions. It is only when you are making statements (preaching or lecturing) that you tread on dangerous ground.

Making the shift
While you may have heard this cop/coach notion before, grasping the concept intellectually will not

change anything. Your organization is not likely to change until your *thinking* actually shifts.

So, for example, even though you may know that trust is an important element in the new workplace, you cannot trust people as a technique. You will only trust people when you truly see people as trustworthy. The shift of perspective is everything.

To use the analogy you will read in the next chapter, I hope to point you to a tree in the middle of your weed patch. I might even be able to show you how to climb that tree to get a different view of your world. But you will have to make the climb yourself.

Once you truly see a bigger picture for yourself and are touched by the simplicity and common sense of what you see, you can effortlessly and painlessly make the leap to this new understanding. You will be out of the weeds and onto the beach . . . forever!

Like most things that are simple, this new model is not always an easy picture to see at first. I promise you it will be worth whatever it takes for you to move into this new reality. I urge you to be curious, keep an open mind, relax and be patient.

The answers you seek will unfold themselves to you when you least expect them.

Part 2

Out of the Weeds

4
Lost in the weeds

For many people, operating a business is like being lost in the jungle. (In the restaurant industry we talk about being lost in the weeds!) When this is what your life is like, you show up every day and hack away at the weeds, trying to keep a clear space to operate.

The work is hot, you get tired and sweaty, your back aches, the bugs bite and you have to keep an eye out for snakes. Still, you can't stop cutting for very long because the weeds grow back quickly whenever you take a break. Does this sound familiar?

In the world of weeds, people are always looking for a better way to cut. Breakthroughs are things like improved cutting technique ("for maximum efficiency, keep your elbow straight and swing from the shoulder . . .") and there is endless debate about cutting implements ("curved blades are better than straight blades . . .")

There are chain saw freaks, napalm advocates, poison promoters and so forth. Everybody has a favorite way to clear the weeds . . . but you are still in the weed-cutting business.

People make careers of studying the different weeds, learning their technical names and researching their growth patterns. There are many weed management programs, each with its supporters and detractors.

Consultants get wealthy showing people new and unusual ways to hack away at their particular set of weeds but in the end, all you have are just different variations on weed-cutting.

Occasionally you may hear some "crazy person" say that weed-cutting skills are unnecessary. This loony may even be so bold as to suggest there is a world without weeds. What madness! As you continue to hack away, you quickly dismiss him as a crackpot who obviously doesn't have a grasp of "reality," all the while cursing the weeds.

You know that weed-cutting is backbreaking work but it is the only world most managers know. With some pride, you may even say you are starting to know the weeds much better and you're developing a really good cutting stroke!

You are spurred on by the naive belief that if you only continue to apply yourself diligently to the task, you will be able to get ahead of the weeds and when you do, everything will work out well.

What are you pretending not to know?

The truth is that nothing much changes in the world of weeds. If you could achieve the kind of enjoyable, productive organization you dream about through enhanced cutting skills, you would already be seeing that sort of result because you are getting really good at weed-cutting.

I once had a manager tell me that he knew what he was doing didn't work, but he didn't want to consider alternatives ideas because he was getting really good at what he was doing! Many managers are getting better and better at doing things that don't work!

Albert Einstein once observed that you can't solve a problem on the level at which it was created. In other words, the thinking that got you *into* a problem is not going to get you *out!*

To apply this to my analogy here, if you ever want to get out of the weed-cutting business, you first have to raise your level. You have to climb a tree.

(Actually, the first breakthrough is to recognize there is even such a thing *as* a tree. In the world of weeds, trees just look like particularly nasty weeds!)

When you are able to go up a tree a bit – when you can see your world from a different perspective – you will clearly see that the weeds only grow in the small area immediately around you. Suddenly you see that next to the weed patch is a beach with a little bar.

Once you see that, your own innate common sense will take over. You clearly see that you could just as easily be sitting in the sun with a frosty beverage – all you have to do is choose to walk out of the weed patch . . . and why wouldn't you do it?

The "crazy folks" were right – you never had to cut weeds in the first place . . . but you couldn't see that for yourself until you allowed your perspective to expand. You were lost and didn't even know it.

Yet even as our hero relaxes on the beach, there are people back in the weeds, hacking away and thinking to themselves, "There's GOT to be an easier way to do this!"

(And if he tried to tell them about the beach, their explanation would be that he had lost his grip on "reality.") Who is crazy?

5
Life on the beach

You know about living in the weeds. What is it like on the beach? To help you understand, here are some comments from one CEO who saw a different picture.

The words are those of Kevin Gleason, CEO of an advertising company in Minneapolis. In the early 80's, the company's owners did what a lot of people did in the early 80's – they leveraged the company, took the money and ran. This left the organization with an incredible debt and while they still had healthy sales, they were having a hard time.

A week after Kevin took over as CEO, the bank phoned to say they were going to call the company's loan! His response was, "give me six months."

(He confessed that he didn't know at the time what he was going to *do* in those six months, but he knew he needed time to do something different!)

Kevin got in touch with the folks who were very instrumental in pointing me in the direction I discuss in this book. Rather than talk about the specifics of how his financial picture changed, perhaps the best way to describe the degree of turnaround is to tell you that a year or so later, Kevin was getting phone calls from the same banker saying, "You know, we have some problem companies in our portfolio. If we lent you the money, would you buy them?"

That is a serious turnaround . . . and this is the way Kevin describes his organization. He says:

Imagine a work place where the environment is calm, yet people are intensely involved in work activities.

Imagine business meetings so enjoyable and productive that people leave more energized than when they arrived.

Imagine managers making decisions based on reflection rather than from fear or by knee jerk reaction to circumstances.

Imagine a work force so resilient that disruptive factors like disappointment and change have but a very temporary effect.

Imagine the energy so often wasted dealing with interpersonal and individual stress being put, instead, into the work itself.

Imagine an environment where there's no concern about motivating people with incentives or pressure since people are generally happy and productive.

Imagine morale at such a high level that staff and managers arrive home from work in a state of mind that actually increases the well-being of the people in their lives, rather than detracting from it.

Imagine an organization that has trust and confidence in its staff, allowing them to be responsible for their own thinking.

Imagine a happy, healthy and productive group of men and women who actualize levels of ability and service which they did not even know they were capable of.

Imagine taking your company to a higher level than you ever dreamed possible through accessing the fundamental innate intelligence of your staff.

How does that sound? If this was honestly an accurate description of the way your company operated, what do you think would be happening for you in the market? What do you think it would be like for your clients to patronize you? What do you think it would be like for your staff to work for your organization?

From my own experience, I can tell you that this picture is not only extremely accurate but it is the way things are supposed to be. All organizations are capable of functioning in this way – it is hardwired into human nature.

The extent to which you are not seeing behavior like this in your company is just the extent to which your own understanding (or lack of it) is getting in the way.

6
Out of the weeds

If you find management to be a struggle, the problem most likely lies in your thinking about what it takes to run your company and your ideas about what you are supposed to be as a manager.

The first step from the weeds to the beach is a willingness to entertain the notion that there are possibilities you haven't seen yet.

One seminar I attended spoke of three possible types of information: the things you know that you know, the things you know that you don't know and the things you don't know that you don't know.

In other words, we all have blind spots, we just don't know where they are (which is, of course, what makes them blind spots!)

You can't reach the beach until you are willing to shine some light into your blind spots. When you can drop judgements and personal ego long enough to open yourself to new insights, you will be amazed at what you can see.

The second step toward a weed-free life is to realize that you don't quite know how to get there from where you are.

If you did, you wouldn't be working so hard or feeling so stressed and you certainly wouldn't be dealing with the types of problems you are dealing with now. It seems that the humility required to honestly admit that you don't have a clue is a major aid to finally seeing the path toward an easier life.

While all this may sound too good to be true, I promise that the beach exists and that you **can** get there. I also stress that making the shift involves increasing your understanding, not your knowledge.

You are looking for what some describe as a blinding flash of the obvious . . . and that will come from a personal insight rather than from linear (reasoned) thinking.

Part 3

A Fresh Look
at Management

7
Control

The job of management is to control the operation, true or false?

Ask this question of most managers and I expect they would agree. This is understandable of course, but I suggest a control attitude is an open invitation to a management career of endless struggle and stress.

The simple truth of the matter is that your operation is out of control! The sooner you realize that and learn to live with it, the easier your life will be!

Control is a myth, because unless you want to sit on somebody's shoulder and tell them what to do second-by-second throughout the day (which is not a great idea, even if it were possible), they will do what makes sense to them in the moment. In that regard, it is entirely out of your control.

Leadership
Somebody once said that "leadership is getting the herd to move roughly west!" and I think that is an accurate description of the reality of it.

Within the parameter of "roughly west" you will have people who are headed straight west at a dead run and you will have some who seem to be milling around. Some days you will move faster than you will on other days, but if the general movement of the organization is toward the west, you are OK.

This means that the job of the leader is to determine in what direction the company should be moving, communicate that direction to the staff and help the company move that way. It is not to enforce a set of rules to preserve the illusion of control.

Strays

Every once in a while, you will have someone who is wandering off to the north. North is a good direction. There is nothing wrong with north, it's just not the direction you chose to have the herd move.

(There is a time for everyone to head off in their own direction. Your job as an effective leader is not to fight that urge, merely to channel it in an appropriate manner.)

When someone in your westbound organization wanders off to the north, you first need to find out if they are disoriented or if they really want to go north. If they are lost, give a little course correction and point them back toward the west. If they are truly northbound, get them in touch with an organization that is moving north. Everyone will be happier!

(For example, hockey great Wayne Gretzky is a skilled athlete, but if you are going to play basketball, Wayne is either going to have to lose the skates . . . or go next door to the rink where he will fit right in!)

Control is a myth and if you are willing to let it go and just keep tabs on what direction things are moving, everything just works more easily!

8

Chris the dishwasher

Often, someone who looks lost may simply be mis-assigned. Here is a personal example that may give you another way to look at performance

When I was in charge of the foodservice department at the Olympic Training Center, I had a dishwasher named Chris. He was a good kid, but he was just not making it in the dishroom and there was a part of me that said if he could not make it there, he had not earned the right to go anywhere else.

Chris had a job history like many that we see in the hospitality industry – three months in one job, six months in another – and it was looking like the OTC was going to be another repeat performance.

Then one day it hit me: Chris was never going to make it in the dishroom because he did not *want* to make it in the dishroom. At that point, I figured I had nothing to lose – he was going to be gone unless I could find something that would work.

I took him aside one day and asked, "Is it obvious to you what is going to happen if we keep going like this?" He acknowledged that he did – he had been through it before. My next question was not what he expected: "It is apparent that you are not going to be good in this job because you really don't *want* to be good in this job. What do you really want to do?"

He thought for a second and replied, "I want to go into the dining room." Figuring I had nothing to lose, I agreed, with the understanding that it was either up or out – if things didn't work out in the dining room, he could not come back into the dishroom. "You just watch me," he said.

The next opening that came up in the dining room went to Chris . . . and he was doing pretty well. The really exciting part, though, was what happened when we got into a project to upgrade our salad bar.

The salad bar breakthrough

A different staff member was responsible for setting up our salad bar every day. My spec on the salad bar was simple. I wanted to hear a spontaneous, positive comment when the athletes took a look at it. If it was your day to do the salad bar and  you weren't hearing any comments, tweak it until you got the reaction we wanted.

I had borrowed videos on garnishing from the local Community College and my crew was learning to make tomato roses and similar fancy touches. Many of the staff were using ideas they had learned from the tapes and we were hearing good comments.

A few days later it was Chris' turn to do the salad bar.

From the time I walked in the door that morning, everyone was saying, "You have to see Chris's salad bar," so I went to see what all the buzz was about.

I immediately saw why they were excited. Chris had designed a beach scene with palm trees and surfers – everything made from fruit and vegetables – and none of which was on the videos! When I asked him about it, he said, "Well, it seemed to me that if A was possible, then you could do B and if you could do B, I didn't see a reason why you couldn't do C!" Chris had caught on fire!

A turning point?

I don't know where Chris is or what he is doing these days, but I believe that event was a turning point in his life. For perhaps the first time in his working history, Chris had discovered he could be good at something on his own terms! It just had to be a breakthrough experience for him!

Someone obsessed with control would probably have handled Chris's poor performance by firing him. If it had played out that way, the OTC would have lost a great worker and Chris would have one more failure to convince himself he wasn't very good at anything. Everybody would have lost.

By looking for a way to help Chris continue to move west with the rest of us, a perfect, if unconventional, solution appeared . . . and everybody won!

9
Your real job

As managers, I believe our real job is not to **run** the joint, it is to teach our **staff** how to run the joint!

You will never be able to move on to new projects (or get away to spend more time with your family) unless your crew can assume responsibilities that presently fall to you . . . and the only way they will be able to do these new jobs is if someone teaches them.

Disrespect
If you are doing anything that someone on your staff is capable of doing – and you are not giving it to them to do, it is disrespectful. You are standing in the way of their professional development. Overtones of disrespect will quickly destroy working relationships in any organization.

Failure to pass down routine tasks may also deliver a message that you do not think the other person is capable of doing the job. (Whether or not that particular conclusion is correct is irrelevant.) Your reluctance to let loose of tasks, especially the simple ones, could be seen as your way of keeping the power in your own hands.

The organization suffers because qualified people leave for jobs where they **can** advance their skills while at the same time, managers perpetuate the job overload that leads to exhaustion, stress and burnout.

Work smarter

Take a look at where you are spending your time. Do you spend hours doing the schedule? There is no law that says you have to do it, only that a schedule needs to be done. If you have it down cold, or if it is driving you crazy, teach someone else on your staff to do it! After all, at some point in your career someone had to trust *you* with the job for the first time. Delegation will be a relief to you and a job upgrade for them.

 The same thinking applies to other typical manager jobs like taking the inventory or doing most ordering. Someone on your staff, with a little coaching, can learn to handle these tasks as well (or better!) than you can . . . and it will not be hard to keep score on how they are doing.

Start with three tasks

As a start, identify three activities that occupy your time – jobs that others on your staff are already capable of doing. If these folks are willing to take on the new responsibilities, give the jobs to them.

Do not insist that they do everything exactly the way you would. All you really need is consistency of the results. If they can get the same or better results without breaking any laws, why waste energy insisting on the manner in which that has to happen?

When you are comfortable that the new tasks are being well-handled, identify three of the common jobs on your list that others in the organization are capable of *learning* and with your newfound free time, start teaching them!

The results of this process are simply wonderful! You take jobs that are wearing you down and give them to people who get excited about them! You continually reinvent your own job which tends to keep you fresh and excited. Your staff will become more confident, more skilled and more involved in the success of your operation.

A few words of caution before you start:

There is a difference between delegation and abdication

Never turn anyone loose unless they have been thoroughly coached or they may panic and fail. As a world-class manager, you want to make sure they succeed in their new work – failure helps no one.

You may want to do a job until you have mastered it before you turn it over to someone else. In some cases, where you know that you just do not have the temperament for a particular task, delegating it to someone who does may work out better for everyone. It is OK if your staff knows more than you do.

Do not delegate to people who do not want the responsibility

Not everyone wants to advance and it is futile to force activity on someone who does not want it. If you have a history of successful transitions and people are comfortable that they won't be set up to fail, they will

37

be more eager to tackle something new, particularly if you reward their achievement.

Reflect the new responsibilities on the check

You have to deal with the question of "what's in it for me?" It is only fair to reflect someone's increased contributions to your profitability on their paycheck. If you don't give for what you get you will not find many volunteers for new duties.

Don't view delegation as increasing costs. Rather, see it as a way to break you loose to identify more ways to increase revenue. Even if delegation does nothing other than give you time to have a life (!), any additional costs will be more than offset by your own increase in productivity.

Expect mistakes

A "mistake" only shows you the extent of a person's understanding. We all slip a few times when taking on new challenges. Since no one likes to fail, making a big deal of an error will only destroy the desire to learn and add another "rule" to the book.

Approach your job as a coach would ("This is good, that is good, let's work on this part now.") and you will do fine. Bear in mind that you, too, are also learning – in this case, how to delegate successfully – and you should expect a mistake or two yourself as you learn how to do it effectively.

Does this mean that things will happen differently than the way you would have done them? Almost certainly. Does this mean that you will not get the results you want? Not at all. The right things will still happen – the herd will continue to move roughly west – but with fresh energy from many other people.

10
The power of presence

The secret to creating impact with others is presence.

Simply put, presence is a state of mind that is free from distraction. Your level of presence is the extent to which your mind is not occupied with thoughts unrelated to the project at hand.

Here are a few examples of what I mean:

Have you ever been talking to someone who was listening to you . . . and then suddenly they **weren't** listening to you? They may even have been looking at you and nodding their heads as you spoke, but didn't you know when their attention was elsewhere?

Have you talked with someone on the phone while they were doing something else at the same time? Even though you couldn't see them, hasn't it been obvious when you did not have their total attention?

These are both instances of a distracted state of mind that results in low presence.

Recall your experience of what it feels like to talk to someone who was not really listening to you. If you are like most people, you probably find that distracted behavior to be rude at best and angering at worst.

Distractions

A distracted state of mind creates irritation in other people. You know how incredibly annoying it can be to talk with someone whose mind has wandered. Yet we do the same thing to people constantly because we have accepted the notion that the way to be efficient and get more done is to do several tasks at once. In fact, effectiveness comes from just the opposite approach.

 Were you ever on the phone while you were working on the schedule and trying to handle a question from one of your staff members at the same time? My guess is that neither the person on the other end of the phone, the schedule or your staff member got the attention they really needed.

In all likelihood you probably had to go back to one or all of these "projects" for clarification, to correct mistakes or to make another try at resolving more "problems" that could easily have been avoided if you were not so distracted the first time.

Lessons from life
Imagine a two-year-old is looking for attention and you are busy. As they tug on your pants leg you say "Later, kid, I'm busy" without looking up from your work. Do they respond "Sure, Daddy, I understand?" Not a chance!

To take care of a two-year-old you have to drop what you are doing, get down eyeball to eyeball and give them your undivided attention for about five seconds. If you do this, you'll buy yourself some time. You may get a few minutes and you may get an hour but if children don't get your complete attention, they will pull on you for the rest of their natural lives!

It is no different if they are twenty-two or sixty-two. People want to know that you "got it." They want to know that what they had to say actually got **through** to you and this cannot happen if you are distracted.

The only difference between dealing with children and adults is that kids are more honest – they will not pretend that they have your attention if your mind is wandering. Adults are usually more socially correct, but they are no less observant.

Presence and productivity
The truth is that you can really only concentrate on one thing at a time anyway. When you are talking with another person, there is nothing you can do at that same moment about finishing the schedule (or your budget, your sick child or your vacation.)

If your mind is preoccupied with extraneous thoughts, your attention is not fully with the person in front of you. Even if they do not call you on it, they will come back again and again trying to get through to you.

As with children, you can handle a situation in five seconds or five hours – the only difference is your level of presence when you do it.

The secret to productivity is to handle things exactly the way you would with a child. Drop distractions, focus your attention, handle one item at a time and move on to the next project. Presence (or lack of distraction) will enable you to more accurately assess the situation and quickly deal with it in a more effective way.

Presence and service

In my service seminars, I point out that the reason guests leave a tip of 10% or 30% depends in large measure on the level of personal connection servers create with their guests.

Presence increases the personal connection between people. In fact, without presence, there can be no personal connection at all.

I watched one server increase his tips from 12% one night to over 30% the next night by, as he said, "just trying to be at the table when I am at the table." I had a manager tell me over half of his "people problems" seemed to disappear when he started becoming aware of (and dropping) distracting thoughts.

When your customers have a complaint or when your staff members have a question, what they want most is to feel that you really *heard* what they had to say. Most people do not expect you to resolve their every concern on the spot, but they want to sense that what they had to say was important to you.

Just as a distracted state of mind creates irritation, presence makes people feel more positive and better-served. You convey your caring by your level of presence and people highly value the message they get when you are in the moment with them. In work with tipped employees (restaurant staff and hair stylists) we found increased presence improved their tips by 250%!

If you have ever worked for someone who did not listen, you know the feeling of being ignored. You can't tell someone who does not listen that they do not listen because, well, they do not listen! People who do not listen really think that they do, so your challenge is to be sure that you are not guilty of the same sin when someone needs your attention.

Presence and enjoyment

There is a direct connection between your level of presence and the enjoyment you derive from what you are doing. Have you ever been so immersed in an activity that you totally lost track of time? If so, you have had the experience of operating in a state of high presence (without distracting thoughts.)

If you find your job irritating, the only problem may be that you are distracted. Clear your head, focus and watch how much fun things will become. Anything worth doing is worth doing . . . with full presence.

A natural state

Presence is not something unnatural. We are all born with high presence. Little babies have high presence because their heads aren't yet cluttered with thoughts – they only know how to deal with what is right in front of them at the moment.

This sounds too simple but what happens when you bring a newborn baby into a room? Everybody's attention shifts to the baby. People start to smile and forget about their own problems for a few minutes. The baby is not **doing** anything – just being there – yet everyone around feels a little better.

This demonstrates the power presence has to make others feel more positive. High presence is our birthright, but it is also something we can easily lose sight of as the pace of business speeds up, our lives become increasingly complex and we take on more "responsibilities."

Start to notice
It is unrealistic to think that you can always operate without distractions, but you can start to be aware of distracting thoughts when they start to clutter your mind. One way to tell this is happening is when the people you are talking with get restless or when you see a glazed look in their eyes. When your attention wanders, so will theirs.

The good news is that simply becoming aware of the fact that you are distracted will start to put you back on track. When you notice that you are becoming distracted, just gently let go of the stray thoughts and let your attention return to the task at hand.

Your increased presence will make whomever you are talking to feel better-served and it will bring more impact to your message.

11
Motivation

Would you think the manager's job is to motivate the staff? If so, you are making your job more difficult.

When most managers talk about motivation, they are typically referring to external motivation. If it is your job to motivate someone, then it must be coming from you to them.

There are basically two ways that you can provide external motivation: one is the carrot and the stick, the other is the gun to the back of the head!

There is no doubt that you can get things done using these two models of motivation . . . but for these models to be effective over time, you will need a larger and larger carrot . . . and you will need to keep getting bigger guns as well!

The other problem is that if this is the only way you can achieve results in your organization, it requires you to be there holding the stick or nothing happens. If you are working 70-80 hours a week, it's probably because you set things up this way.

Human relations consultant Robert Kausen makes these observations:

> "People naturally want to produce excellent results. Contrary to popular misconception, employees really do want to work, and they instinctively want to produce top notch results. When we excel, we feel wonderful. When we throw ourselves into our work, we experience a natural high that inspires us to do even better.
>
> High performance feels wonderful and holding back is no fun. It is the total involvement, not the activity, that results in the enjoyment. The enemy of involvement is distraction. You cannot quiet someone's distracted mind, but you can provide a sane climate that promotes healthy mental functioning, thus greater involvement and impact."

Does that sound like a little more workable model of motivation? If so, let's look at it in more detail.

12
Climate

There's a relationship between climate and motivation – or any behavior, for that matter – and if you can understand how they interrelate, it will make a major difference in your ability to influence results.

The model below shows the relationship between the climate in the organization, the feeling on the job and what you tend to see for behavior at various levels.

ORGANIZATIONAL BEHAVIOR

CLIMATE	FEELING ON THE JOB	ORGANIZATIONAL BEHAVIOR	
EXHILARATION	*Effortless*	Intuitive	Creativity
		Magic	Self-Management
		Synergy	Customer Delight
INSPIRATION	*Alive*	Teamwork	Productivity
		Initiative	Motivation
		Clarity	Professional Curiosity
CONTENTMENT	*Hopeful*	Flexibility	Confidence
		Cooperation	Humorous
		Extra Effort	Attention to Detail
TENSION	*Stressed*	Gossip	Whining & Complaining
		Tardiness	Defensiveness
		Distrust	Resistance to Change
UNHAPPINESS	*Upset*	Suspicion	No-Shows
		Accidents	Cliques
		Turnover	Disagreements
CHAOS	*Frightening*	Fights	Theft
		Subversion	Arguments
		Anger	Walk-Outs

Below the line behavior

If a company has a very low climate – call it chaos – the feeling on the job is absolutely frightening. The behavior you tend to see in an organization at that level is fights, theft, anger and walkouts. If you have ever worked in an organization that was running in chaos, you know that it is terrifying!

As it gets a little bit better, maybe you reach a point of unhappiness. The feeling on the job is upset and what you tend to see for behavior is turnover and cliques. In a corporate situation, you see people hoarding information and building empires. Turnover is high because people do not want to hang out with you. It is better than chaos, but it is still dysfunctional behavior.

A lot of businesses, particularly restaurants, run in tension. The feeling on the job is stressed and the behavior you are likely to see is gossip, distrust, complaining and petty sniping. Again, organizational functioning has improved, but you are still below the line and unproductive.

Above the line behavior

As you get above the line, you start to get into more productive thinking. Contentment starts to come back in. Hope starts to come back in. You start to see spontaneous, positive humor (as opposed to that negative joke-at-your-expense kind of humor.) The organization starts to lighten up.

As it gets even better, you reach a level we might call inspiration. The feeling in the company is alive. You will see teamwork. You start to see natural, internal motivation and high productivity.

A very high climate – call it exhilaration – produces a feeling of effortlessness on the job. What you see in the organization is creativity, magic and people managing themselves.

In a positive climate you see a high level of customer service because the feeling is rather like being in love. You don't have to talk to somebody in love about taking care of people – people in love take care of people cause they just want to do it.

In a positive climate you will naturally get teamwork, caring and motivation; in a negative climate, good luck! A positive climate will produce total quality management by default; in a negative climate, TQM is going to be one more failed program.

The key to understanding organizational behavior lies in grasping that behavior is merely a very predictable symptom of the work environment. To change work performance, change the work environment.

13
The day from Hell

The notion that behavior in the organization is simply a reflection of the climate is so simple and yet revolutionary when we compare it to the way we always thought things worked. Because I know this idea can seem too simple to be applicable in the real world, let me describe a personal example to illustrate the power of this understanding:

In the mid 1980s, I was hired by the US Olympic Committee to run the foodservice at the Olympic Training Center (OTC) in Colorado Springs. The OTC is a year-round operation whose dining program at the time was in desperate need of major surgery. In fact, foodservice had consistently been the leading source of complaints from the athletes about their training experience.

How low can you go?
To underscore how bad things were, the day I arrived to take over the dining operations we had two knife fights in the kitchen!

Apparently, two of my workers got into an argument and were waving kitchen knives at each other with some degree of seriousness. No damage was done, everyone was nervous for a few minutes. This had all the signs of being a real "Day from Hell"!

I had received some excellent training up to that point in my professional career but nowhere had I received any instruction in how to deal with knife fights!

I hope you never encounter a predicament like this in your own operation but it could be an interesting case study. For a moment, put yourself in my position and imagine how you might have approached a situation like this.

The classic approach
In the old "management expertise" (cop-based) mode that I spent so many years refining, my first response to this predicament would likely have been to fire – or at least suspend or put on probation – the people involved. After all, it is important to deliver a clear message that this is unacceptable behavior, right?

After that, if I didn't already have one, I would have written a clear policy about knife fights. It would have specified that engaging in such dangerous behavior was unacceptable conduct and could be considered grounds for immediate dismissal.

Finally, I would have held a special staff meeting to explain the policy. I would have made sure my staff understood how behavior of this sort worked against everything we were trying to accomplish. I would have talked about the importance of teamwork and cooperation, probably with some Olympic analogies.

I would have shared my vision for the operation and tried to get my crew excited about what we could do together. It would have been an inspirational session designed to help my staff see that we were all in this together and we had to work together to succeed in providing memorable service to the athletes.

What's wrong with this picture?

I share this story in many of my seminars. When we reach this point in the discussion, the majority of managers generally agree that they would probably take an approach similar to the one I just described.

My next question to them (and to you) is this:

> *"How effective do you think this strategy would be at eliminating knife fights forever and always in your operation?"*

Somewhat sheepishly, the managers usually confess that while there might be some short term effect, they don't really expect that much would change.

The conversation usually sounds like this:

> *"Is this more or less what you would do?"*
> *"Well . . . yes."*
> *"Would it work?"*
> *"Well . . . no."*
> *"But it's still about the way you would handle it?"*
> *"Well . . . yes."*

Do you see the problem?

Now had I followed this scenario when the situation arose, this strategy would not have worked either. Worse yet, when I didn't get the results I wanted, I would have looked at how to write a better memo or how to hold a more effective staff meeting!

I would worry that perhaps I didn't come down on them fast enough and hard enough. It would never have occurred to me that approaching the problem in this manner was a futile exercise from the very beginning. This is what I mean about becoming better and better at doing things that don't work!

Applying a new understanding

When the knife fights came up, however, I had arrived at a different understanding about the real cause of behavior. I had started to recognize that behavior was just a symptom of a person's level of thinking as reflected in the climate of the organization.

Instead of seeing the knife fight as a statement about the people involved, I saw it as the indication of a low climate. The workers involved in the incident were simply in a state of mind where swinging knives at each other seemed like an appropriate way to settle a dispute. I understood that the only way the behavior would change was when the level of thinking that created it changed.

In this case, I talked with the two combatants and probably suggested that carving up their co-workers was inappropriate and dangerous, but I never addressed the fight directly. Instead, my conversation went something like this:

"Given what happened, it is obvious to me that something has you really frustrated. What's wrong with this chicken outfit? What's making your job tough and what do you think we can do about it?"

My goal was to **listen** – not for hard facts, but for an insight into what was weighing heavily on their minds. Whatever the preoccupation was, it was making their lives (and mine!) more difficult, affecting their thinking and leading to their unproductive behavior.

Accomplishing this goal just required that I listen without judgement – be "dumb as dirt" if you will. I had learned that the simple act of nonjudgmental listening was a major aid in helping people return to a healthier state of mind.

I knew the behavior would change when their level of personal security and well-being increased. In a higher state of mind, the notion of attacking someone else would not even occur to them. The behavior was not a problem. It was a symptom.

Learn from your staff
My discussions were revealing. I quickly discovered we had many more people on staff than we needed. Activity at the OTC was very seasonal at that point and my predecessor had not trimmed the staff from its peak summer levels.

All he did was cut everyone's hours back. They were not making enough money to live on, but they could not afford to quit their jobs. Under these conditions, I would have been frustrated, too!

This is not management by meditation
It became obvious that to eliminate the frustration I had to eliminate the problem of lack of hours. I held a series of one-on-one interviews to get some sense of my new workers as individuals and to see what was on their minds. Then I resolved the hours issue the only way I could. I fired half my crew!

I placed on my termination list those whom I believed were the most negative or angry (in the lowest states of mind) but on a different day it might well have been a different group of people. Even if *everyone* had been in a great mood, I *still* would have let half of them go!

"OK, we all have full hours, so that's not an issue. What's the next thing we have to work on?" (As an interesting side note, the knife-fighters were among the people I kept on the team!)

I admit "Black Wednesday," the day I trimmed the staff, was nobody's idea of a good time . . . but when it was over, it was over. After the initial shock of the staff reduction passed, everyone immediately felt better. The whiners and complainers were gone and all who remained had a full schedule.

With the issue of adequate hours eliminated, the general work climate improved. In a more positive state of mind, people suggested other areas that could be corrected. When we uncovered an irritant, we fixed it. Every time we eliminated a distraction, the climate became more positive.

Some interesting things happened

The next day, not only had knife fights stopped, but the idea would not even enter anyone's mind! In fact, we never talked about knife fights again and we never had a similar incident again.

There were some other interesting benefits of this approach: Within about two months, foodservice had become the number one source of compliments from the athletes and coaches – all the more remarkable because this happened with the same workers who had made us the number one source of complaints!

Over the next six months, dining room patronage nearly doubled. At the same time, our labor cost per meal dropped more than 20 percent and our cost per meal declined nearly 25 percent. Staff turnover went from 300 percent to 25 percent without a change in wage rates!

Almost five years later when I left the OTC, the original people involved in the knife fights were still on staff and were among our most productive workers . . . and most people would have thrown them away!

Behavior is only a symptom

I share this story to illustrate the power that comes from understanding how the climate in a company determines the behavior on the job. At the time the knife fight issue came up, I could not have told you for sure if handling things in this manner would succeed . . . but I was certain that "kicking butt and taking names" would fail.

It is important not to think of this story as an essay on how to handle knife fights but merely as an anecdote that shows how one person applied the principles of climate and behavior to a real-life business problem.

The power does not lie in the technique but rather in the understanding. I promise if you truly understand the principles at work, you will instinctively know what to do. Not only that, but your approach is likely to work every time!

There are several management qualities that can improve the climate and lead to self-motivation in the organization. In the next few chapters we will look at a few of them.

14
Listen

One of the best things you can do to improve the climate is to listen. Listen with curiosity, listen with humility, listen for an insight.

(Most people don't listen, they just wait their turn to talk . . . some don't even wait!)

Phillips mentor program
Probably the best example of a structured listening program came out of a management retreat that I facilitated for Phillips Seafood Restaurants, a group of high volume operations in the Chesapeake Bay area.

The meeting's theme was "Phillips in the Year 2000" – what should the organization look like in the next century? Somebody said, "Phillips in the year 2000 is a people company." I responded, "Well, that sounds good . . . but what does a people company *look* like? If this were a people company, how could we tell it from an organization that *wasn't* a people company?"

We kicked this around in the group and came up with what they called a mentor program. Everybody on the hourly staff was assigned a member of management to be a mentor for them – rather like a big brother or sister. Ideally this was not their supervisor. Phillips is a big organization and every manager had about 30 people reporting to them for this purpose.

The staff was guaranteed 30 minutes a month of uninterrupted one-on-one time with their mentor to talk about whatever **they** wanted to talk about. It was not to be a training session or a sermon from the mount. They already had ways to do that.

Some of you are probably going into overload right now and you can imagine that some of the managers were starting to have a little trouble with the idea as well. Thirty people at half an hour apiece is 15 hours a month. The managers were thinking, "Where am I going to find 15 hours a month? I'm already working too many hours as it is."

Mark Sneed. their Operations VP put it in perspective. He said, "If this is what we say we are as a company, this **is** what we are as a company. You have an option of staying with the company, but if this is what we agree to do, you do not have an option of whether or not you are going to participate in this program."

I talked to Mark about six months later to find out how it was going. He said the first couple of months were a bit shaky. However, he said now that the program was implemented, he would lose all of their managers and most of their staff if he tried to eliminate it!

"Without question, it's the best single thing we ever

did," he said. I asked him how the managers found time for the mentoring meetings. He said they had all kinds of time now because when they looked at what had been occupying them in the past, they realized they spent most of their time putting out fires.

"We just don't see those problems anymore," he said. "If Michael graduates in June, we'll know in February what Michael is going to do in June because we're talking to him all the time. Turnover has gone way down, productivity has gone way up and certainly the climate on the job has improved immensely."

"We got all the things we expected to get," he went on. "What we got that we did not expect was that our level of customer service has improved measurably. Maybe because our staff has a model of one-on-one interaction with their managers, they deal with the guests one-on-one."

What did you learn from your staff today?
To make a major improvement in your operation, all you have to do is sit down with your crew one on one and ask, "What's wrong with this chicken outfit? What's making your job tough? What can I do to help you be more successful?" Then shut up and listen.

You don't have to have an opinion about what they tell you. For example, somebody could say, "I want to eat my dog." You can entertain the idea, even understand why that idea might make sense to them – without having to agree, disagree or even express an opinion at all.

15
The benefit of the doubt

Maybe this is just another way to listen, but maintain a benefit-of-the-doubt stance with your staff. Assume the best until you have all the facts. Understand that there is always more information than you have.

If Karen has been late three times and is late again, it is easy to jump to a conclusion about Karen. But maybe this is the day her child got hit by a car and she's had a few other things on her mind.

I don't know the details, but I know that Karen would not have been late unless Karen had a reason *that made sense to Karen.* The fact that it may or may not make sense to me is not required. I want to find out what that reason is before I make up my mind. It doesn't mean I will buy her story, but I want to hear it before I decide how to proceed.

What you think is what you get
It is interesting that when you assume the best, you tend to get it. I know when I saw my staff as a bunch of crooks who'd rob me blind if I didn't watch them every minute, I was not disappointed.

And when I saw them as intelligent adults who wanted to make a contribution if they just had an opportunity to do that, I wasn't disappointed either.

In some cases, they were the same people.

16
Serve your staff

The analogy that comes to mind is the Canadian sport of curling. I would describe it as shuffleboard on ice. One member of the team gives a heavy stone a push down the ice toward a target while two other team members move along ahead of the stone, sweeping the ice with brooms.

The sweepers have two jobs: to get everything out of the way of the stone that might impede its progress and to make sure that the stone has a totally clean sheet of ice to run on. Depending on whether they sweep faster or slower, they make the ice a little faster or slower and that determines how far the stone is going to go. But the momentum and direction are already established by somebody else.

Like the stone, your organization has a momentum – it is moving in a direction. As the manager, I'd rather be up in front with the broom, eliminating everything that might throw the stone off course than in the back, trying to push the stone through all the debris.

The manager's traditional job has been to push the company through any obstacles that lie in its path. The new model recognizes that businesses have their own momentum. The proper focus of management should be to keep that energy flowing unimpeded rather than trying to force the movement.

17
Value and respect

Value and respect your crew. On one level, think of what it would be like if everybody walked out on you in the middle of your busiest rush period. But on an entirely different level, when you allow yourself to connect with your staff as human beings, you will be moved by their innocence and heroism.

Everyday heroism
I think it is heroic for a single mother to raise three children. I think it is heroic to be sixteen – it is a lot harder job now than it was when we did it! When you allow yourself this human connection, you will start treating people well because you will see that they deserve the best level of care you can muster.

You have people on your staff who are up against some amazing challenges. They've got family problems, money problems and many other struggles in their lives, but they show up every day and do the best they can. When you get touched by that, you start to take good care of them because they are worth it. When you deal with them that way, they will tend to deal with your customers that way. When you deal with them that way, you create a more positive climate.

18
A free and clear mind

The most potent thing you bring to the job is your own mental health. Remember that the climate of the organization always starts at the top. The reason you cannot regularly work 60 or more hours a week is that your mind gets scrambled, your own level of well-being drops and the productivity of the entire organization suffers.

This is part of radical concept called Have a Life!

If hard work made money, you would be among the richest people on the planet! You got where you are based on what you could **do**, but your future success will be based on what you can **get done**.

Anything you are doing right now, someone on your staff is capable of doing or eventually learning how to do . . . but the only thing you can't give away is the vision – your sense of what your company could be. Vision is clarity about what "west" looks like in your organization and vision comes from a quiet mind.

So you must be sure to give yourself some quiet time. If that's playing with the kids, do it. If puttering in the garden or getting out on the golf course quiets your mind down, it is appropriate business activity for you (. . . and you can tell your boss I said so!)

Clearing your mind

Rufus Pritchard is a client and friend who owns a restaurant in Nags Head, North Carolina. Rufus loves to play golf but he never played as often as he wanted because he has a very busy restaurant and he felt bad about being gone.

The first time I worked with his managers, I asked his staff what it was like when Rufus went to play golf. They said, "Oh, it's *so* nice!"

"By the time he realizes he's got to get out of here, he is such a pain in the butt. When he leaves, we can actually get some work done. Then he comes back and he's in such a great mood. He's got all these marvelous ideas, and he's so appreciative of us. It's just fantastic!"

So while you are thinking you can't leave, your staff is probably thinking, "Why doesn't he go home?"

As a footnote, Rufus is catching on. He's playing golf regularly now and his restaurants – he has opened a second one – are running better than ever!

19
Support your staff

In the long term, the only way your organization can succeed is if your staff succeeds. This sounds obvious but somehow we got the idea that we could succeed over the bodies of our staff.

Perhaps that came from the days when it seemed like we had disposable labor, when we could treat people any way we wanted to because when they burned out or quit, we had a line of people waiting for their job! You may have noticed the labor market is not like that anymore!

When you select people to become part of your staff, it should represent a commitment on the part of the company (supported by your words and deeds) to encourage and support their development, personally and professionally.

If you are not comfortable about making that level of commitment to an individual, you should not bring that person on board.

20

Tap the power of the climate

A compassionate leader understands that staff members are always doing exactly what makes sense to them given their state of mind at the moment and their conditioned thinking. Negative attitudes and poor performance are just innocent conduct, not willful treachery.

Management becomes an easier, more enjoyable game to play when you respect the power of climate. Instead of cluttering your head with new techniques, all you need to do is understand what affects the climate. Then you implement more of the things that foster goodwill and trust and eliminate practices that contribute to fear and insecurity.

Almost everything you want to happen in your company will happen practically on its own in a positive climate.

Teamwork will happen. Productivity will happen. Exceptional service and caring will happen. If that sounds too easy, then you're on the right track.

Organizations have moods, too

When I would hear whining and complaining at the OTC (and it would happen), it would be a reminder that I had been spending too much time in the office.

So I would make it a point to talk with my staff to find out what they needed, notice things that were going well and make a point to compliment them on their progress. The climate would improve and the negative behavior would disappear.

In a high climate, many of the problems you spend your time dealing with now will probably not show up. (Well, perhaps they will, but in a high climate, problems just look like one more thing to handle.)

If you had an emergency and it just looked like one more thing to handle, do you think your staff would consider it an emergency or not?

21
Set a personal example

The suggestion you probably didn't want to hear is that you have to set a personal example. You cannot go out there, kick butt, take names and then say "Go love the customers." It is not going to work. You are the role model whether you want that job or not.

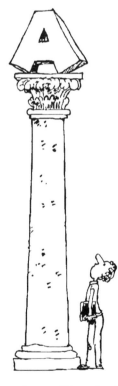

If you want your staff to show up on time, you have to show up on time. Do you want them to dress well? Dress well. Do you want them to listen? Listen. Do you want them to be open to new ideas? Be open to new ideas.

It also helps to realize that the way you treat your staff is the way they will treat your customers. When you lose it, the whole place loses it. When you are stressed out, the whole place becomes stressed out.

When the atmosphere in your business is calm and your staff is attentive and relaxed, your patrons want to return more often. That feeling also improves the climate and makes the company a more attractive place to work.

22
What's your problem?

I know, you don't have problems, you only have challenges. You might say they are not problems, they are opportunities.

I acknowledge that it is less paralyzing to think of opportunities rather than problems, but whatever euphemisms you use, you are still left with a problem in drag! I wonder if the wording ever appreciably changes things for most people.

However, problems (challenges, opportunities or whatever) are a daily fact of life and dealing with them seems to define the job of most managers. So let's take another look at problems, not from a cosmetic point of view but with an eye toward reaching a different understanding of what is and what is not really a problem.

Problems
As a start, a problem is merely a situation that you don't yet have a handle on. Think about that for a minute.

The only reason you would look at a situation as a problem is that you just cannot quite see how to deal with it. Certainly if you knew how to handle it, you would not be likely to think of it as a problem. A nuisance, perhaps, but not really a problem.

If you are honest with yourself, you have to admit that virtually all of the situations you face in life, personal or professional, ultimately have a workable solution. So when something looks like a dilemma, all you are really facing is an event where the answer is not yet apparent to you. You know there is a solution, you just have to figure out how and where to find it. So there really is no problem.

Conditions

A situation where there is no possible resolution, is not a problem, it is a condition.

For example, gravity is a condition. You can love gravity or you can hate it but you are not going to change it! Because gravity is a condition, you are wise to just accept it and devote your energies to pursuits more productive than complaining about it.

What other "problems" do you face every day (and waste time getting upset about) that are, in fact, really conditions? Government regulations? Business seasonality? Taxes? Getting older?

Telling the difference

You may well ask how you can tell what is a condition and what is a problem. If making the distinction is important to you, you will love Chapter 30!

23
Problem-solving

Do you define your job as being a problem-solver? Countless managers do. "Find things that are wrong and fix them" is the order of the day for many, perhaps even most, managers.

The sentiment is admirable but have you noticed what you get when you define yourself as a problem-solver? That's right – you get problems!

In fact, when you define yourself as a problem-solver, you **need** problems to justify your existence so you can feel you are earning your keep. You may even consciously look for them (and they are never hard to find.) Even worse, you may actually encourage people to bring you their problems so you can "do your job."

Now solving problems is certainly better than not solving problems, but every time someone brings you a problem and you take it on, you actually cause the operation to move backwards . . . or at least prevent it from moving forward. Let me explain what I mean:

Gaining Experience

The odds are you already have skill in resolving a wide range of operating problems. In fact, you may pride yourself on your depth of experience . . . and you should. But when you assume the role of problem-solver, you don't often learn anything new – after all, you already know how to solve the problem. Solving repetitive problems is not likely to be a learning experience for you, just a chance to show off a bit and make yourself feel useful.

The bigger danger when you take the stance of problem-solver is that you deprive your staff of an opportunity to learn for themselves what you learned by trial and error over the years. In fact, when you take over, you are actually standing in the way of their professional development.

Anything you are doing is a task they will eventually have to learn in order to advance. When you take charge, the only thing your staff gets trained to do is to bring their problems to you. The next time a similar problem comes up, you get another task laid at your feet . . . and they can take a cigarette break! What's wrong with this picture?

If this is your idea of a good time, have at it. But I suggest that the practice is detrimental to the well-being of your organization . . . and hazardous to your own mental health as well.

Have a life!

The complaint I most often hear voiced by managers is that the hours are too long and they don't have a life. If you don't have a life because you are working long hours in a perpetual problem-solving mode, who do you think the culprit is? It is not the business itself, it is just your own belief that the manager's job is to solve problems!

Let me take some pressure off and suggest that the manager's real job is not to **solve** the problems but to **find** the solutions; not to **have** the answers, but to be able to **find** the answers.

Note that there is nothing in these definitions that requires that the manager be the one to wrestle with every problem that arises. Barring the occasional major disaster, your job as a manager is to help the staff learn how to solve their own problems . . . and that requires that you decline to take on any issue that properly should be handled by someone else in the organization.

If not the manager, who?

To determine who should have the responsibility for finding an answer to any given problem, ask yourself two questions:

> *Whose behavior has to change in order for this issue to be resolved?*
>
> *Whose performance is most affected by this problem?*

The answers to these two questions will point you directly to the person or persons who should tackle the problem.

24
Finding the solution

If you will permit me another restaurant example to illustrate this point, perhaps it will help you grasp what I am getting at. You have been to restaurants enough to understand the situation and I am sure you can find parallels in your own workplace.

Where's my drink?
Let's say you are getting complaints that it is taking a long time for drinks to arrive at the table. Whose problem is it?

In the typical management model, the manager sees it as her problem to solve. If she takes the problem on, she will have to make sure she really knows the intimate realities of what everyone's job is like – an extremely difficult task.

Then she will have to formulate a realistic approach to solve the problem, get all the members of the staff to buy in (or force it down their throats), then follow up to make sure that everyone does what they are "supposed" to do to implement the solution.

It is a lot of thankless work.

This will likely tie her up for days or even weeks . . . and there will still be no guarantee that the company will truly have a handle on the problem.

Plan B

But let's work on the slow drink issue with the idea that the manager's job is only to be able to *find* the answer. In this scenario, the first question is whose behavior has to change?

It could be the bartender . . . or there could be a glitch in the way drinks are ordered or delivered, making servers the likely parties.

Next, whose performance is most affected? It may be the bartender, the cocktail servers or the dining room servers.

By answering two simple questions, you have just identified a group of people who are not only invested in finding an answer to the slow drinks question, but who can actually implement the solution once they agree on what it is . . . and none of them is the manager!

It is their problem to solve. Put them in a room, turn them loose and see what they come up with. You may be surprised at the wisdom and insight they will show once they are trusted to find their own answers.

25
Give your job away

All the great pilot training in the world will never made anyone a great pilot. At some point they have to solo!

If you never give your staff the chance to solo – the chance to test their own ideas without a manager second-guessing and pre-approving every move – they never find out how good they are. They will continue to bring every little decision to you for action or approval.

Putting the responsibility back on your staff to find their own answers may slow things down a bit in the beginning, but it took you awhile (and probably a few spectacular failures) to develop the skills you have today. Don't deprive your staff of the opportunity to make their own mistakes.

Besides, they couldn't mess it up any worse than *you* did when you were first learning, could they?

I am not suggesting the inmates should run the asylum. The job of the manager is still to assure the company is proceeding smoothly in the right direction, but this is not the same as the manager doing all of it by herself.

In fact, the less essential management is to resolving the issues of the day – the more that problem-solving is encouraged and supported at the staff level – the smoother the operation will run and the happier the staff will be!

Back at the Olympics

Here is another example from the OTC to illustrate the point: Within a week after my arrival, my staff was doing almost everything that my predecessor had taken on as his job.

He had been coming in at 5:00am every day to do the ordering. I looked at that and said, a) I don't know how to order for this operation, b) I don't want to do the ordering and, c) I'm not the best person to handle ordering even if I knew how and wanted to do it!

I asked my chef if he would like to handle it . . . and I thought he was going to hug me! He said, "I spend half my day cleaning up the messes that [the old manager] makes because he doesn't know what I have and he doesn't know what I need."

I told him I had no problem with his taking over the ordering as long as we could maintain certain cost relationships and inventory turn. He said, "Just show me how we can keep track of that."

In a flash, I was largely unemployed! Now that I had more time, I looked around for other opportunities and hit on catering. Actually, it was more like the catering idea jumped on me!

Catering

The OTC complex is also the headquarters of the US Olympic Committee and about half the sports in the country so there were always coaches conferences and other events going on. The catering for these was handled primarily by outside caterers because the reputation of OTC foodservice was so bad.

The state of catering became very apparent to me about two days after I arrived when we did a small party for the judo team. Because I was so involved in other activities, I had not been part of the planning for the party but when I took a look at it, I was shocked!

It was a totally amateur effort. I still remember seeing a bag of chips lying on the bar. I asked the person who was putting the party together where the basket was and got a blank stare! When I suggested that we could put the chips in a basket, he got excited! "Wow," he said, "that would really be neat!" Formal catering was taking the Doritos out of the bag!

I saw catering as an opportunity, not only to save money for the sponsoring organizations, but to break up the routine and provide a creative outlet for my staff. A friend who was a superb caterer showed us a direction and we developed a catering program so good that it eliminated the need for outside vendors!

Passing the baton

I ran the parties for a year and a half before I started getting bored with it. I went to one of my supervisors and asked if she would like to take over catering. She said, "I'd love to, but I don't understand it that well."

I suggested that she work with me for a couple of months. Once she understood what I was doing **and why it made sense to me to do it that way,** she was on her own and could do anything she wanted to. We spent a few months together, she got up to speed and I gave her the job. She went off and did things I never even thought about! She blew me away!

I continued to handle the catering bookings until one day I realized that, too, was unproductive. All I was doing was taking the information from the sponsor and relaying it to the kitchen. I asked the kitchen if they would prefer to handle the bookings directly and they said it would really be easier. "Often the sponsor asks us a question and we don't know what you told them." So I gave away the bookings, too.

At the end of my time with the Olympics, I was getting rave reviews on parties I didn't even know we did!

Over the course of nearly five years at the OTC, I effectively gave my job away at least three times. Each period of "unemployment" allowed my to see possibilities that moved the department into new and exciting directions . . . and kept my own interest and enthusiasm high!

26
Flying solo

Some of my colleagues observed that often when there were major parties going on, I was not there. Because their model of management was so different, they accused me of not caring.

On the contrary, I cared intensely – and my staff knew I cared intensely – but I cared enough to give them a chance to find out how good they were without me looking over their shoulders every minute. That is the only way they would ever really solo. If they needed me, they knew they could always reach me, but it was up to them to make the call.

When I first got to the OTC, I would get calls at night and on the weekends. (Certainly if the place is on fire, I want to be perhaps the *second* call they make!) But most of the calls were pretty routine.

When they would call, I might say, "If I was at a movie and you couldn't find me, do you have an idea of what you might do?" They would usually respond that they did. My response was, "Well then, give it a try and see how it works. We'll talk about it Monday." After awhile they stopped calling.

Your staff already knows what to do when they call you – all they are trying to do is cover their butts!

27

How rules are made

Some of the most powerful management concepts are also the most simple. Here is a "blinding flash of the obvious" for your consideration:

The odds are that you are living with behavior today that results directly from some long-forgotten incident involving a member of your staff who left your employ years ago. You see, every time you chew out one of your crew, you add a new "rule" to your company's unwritten code of conduct.

Nobody likes to be yelled at, so when it happens, you create a very uncomfortable situation. Since you can count on people to avoid pain, the word will travel fast. Not only will there be an impact on all your current staff, but as new people are hired, your veteran workers will tell them, "Oh, make sure you never . . ." and they won't.

But what was the story behind the flare-up that started this paranoia? It could have been a simple misunderstanding, a harmless difference of opinion or an isolated incident. Perhaps you were just under stress and overreacted. In the end, the exact circumstances really don't matter. You blew your top about something and the "rule" resulting from that upset will continue to be passed along.

This new "rule" will never show up in your operations manual and it is unlikely that any of your staff will ever discuss it with you. (After all, *you* are the one who so clearly expressed your disapproval, so it is obvious how you feel about it!) Still, the fallout from the incident will influence everyone's behavior for years.

So be careful what you say and how you say it. Be alert for rumors and potential misunderstandings. If you even suspect that something is being taken out of context, address it immediately. If you make a mess, clean it up. If you make a mistake, do what you would want your staff to do if one of *them* made a mistake – apologize, learn from it and move on.

Better yet, conduct yourself in such a way that your actions cannot be misinterpreted. Model the behavior you want to see from your staff. Don't lose your temper. Listen. Watch your tone of voice. Reward progress instead of punishing lapses.

Conduct your counseling sessions in private and never when you are angry. As much as possible, create standards of performance rather than rules. Expect the best and don't jump to conclusions. It is all a human equation, after all.

28
Sound familiar?

To reinforce my previous point, here is an amazing bit of trivia concerning shaping behavior in apes. Now I doubt that you will be training too many primates (although some days it may seem like it!), but see if there is anything in here that strikes a chord with you:

Start with a cage containing five apes. In the cage, hang a banana on a string and put stairs under it. Before long, an ape will go to the stairs and start to climb toward the banana. As the ape touches the stairs, spray all the apes in the cage with cold water.

After awhile, when another ape makes an attempt, spray all the apes with cold water again. Quickly the apes realize that if any of them approaches the stairs, all of them will be sprayed with cold water!

Turn off the cold water. Later, if any other ape tries to climb the stairs, the remaining apes will try to stop him, even though no cold water is sprayed on them.

Now, remove one ape from the cage and replace it with a new one. The new ape will see the banana and try to climb the stairs. To his horror, all of the other apes attack him! After another attempt and attack, he knows that if he tries to climb the stairs, he will be assaulted and he will never try it again.

Next, remove another of the original five apes and

replace it with a new one. The newcomer will go to the stairs and be attacked. The previous newcomer will take part in the punishment with enthusiasm.

Replace a third original ape with a new one. The new ape makes it to the stairs and is attacked as well. Two of the four apes that beat him have no idea why they were not permitted to climb the stairs or why they participated in the beating of the newest ape, but that will not stop their participation.

After replacing the fourth and fifth original apes, all the apes that had once been sprayed with cold water will be gone, yet none of the apes will ever approach the stairs again.

Why not? "Because that's the way it's always been done around here!"

The lesson here is that group behavior will tend to reinforce and perpetuate itself, even in the absence of prior consequences.

What behavior exists around your place that is no longer supported by either necessity or the expressed desires of management? . . . and where such behavior exists, what do you plan to do about it?

29
Lazy people

Do you have any lazy people in your organization? If you do, treasure them! Lazy people will find out how to get things done with the least possible work!

I swear, I love lazy people. They will find a way to do jobs in half the time that it takes you!

This almost sounds silly, but it is true. After all, why would you spend 20 hours doing something if it could be done equally well in 12? (Because you have always done it that way?)

Taking advantage of you staff's natural tendency to do as little work as possible requires a high degree of respect for their innate intelligence, a focus on results and a willingness to have things happen in a different way than you would have done it.

It doesn't sound too difficult when you look at it that way. After all, your job is not to do it, just to see that it gets done.

30
Moving the company

To simplify your life and move your company forward, you need to understand thought. When it comes to thought, all most people a:e aware of is the **content** of their thoughts – good thoughts are better than bad thoughts. Program your mind with happy thoughts and you'll have a happy life.

That misses the point.

The thing to understand is not **what** you are thinking but **how** you are thinking. There are two distinct modes, or ways, of thinking. Let's explore them.

Memory mode
One mode of thinking is memory-based. Memory is the sum and substance of all the things that have happened to you in your life (and what you made up to explain them!) Memory includes all the things your Mom told you that you believed as well as all the things you learned (or decided for yourself) in church, in school and on the playground.

Memory is comprised of all the experiences of your life. It is essentially what is programmed into the data base of your personal in-head computer. Whatever is there can be retrieved, but the information may or may not correlate to the facts of any current situation.

Memory has value . . but it is all old stuff!

I do not mean to bad-mouth memory – it has a place. In repetitive situations where all the variables are known, memory-based thinking is very helpful. If you did not have access to memory, every day you would have to relearn how to drive a car or how to run your computer or your kids' names. (. . . and they like it a lot when you remember who they are!)

When you are thinking in the memory mode, you are actively searching your database for information. It is a bearing-down type of activity. When you are in your memory, you are very attached to your thoughts and everything you know seems like a priceless gem.

Solving problems in the memory mode, is a process of analysis – you sort and re-sort old data, looking for new answers. If you have ever found yourself repeating patterns in your life or had a feeling of "been there, done that," you have experienced the result of busy-minded thinking – you were caught in your own memory, recycling old ideas.

However, busy-minded thinking is not of much help when you are faced with situations where all of the variables are **not** known. When you try to deal with new situations in the memory mode, you must try to interpret new events based on what you know from old events, which only keeps you stuck, repeating past patterns and making the same mistakes.

If you deal with other people from memory, it creates a problem. When you deal with a new situation in the memory mode, either the situation is in your database or it's not. If you find a parallel in memory, the other person is "right." If you cannot find a compatible bit of data, then the other person is "wrong!"

If I jump to a conclusion about what you are saying as soon as you start to talk , if I think, "Oh, I know where this is going," then I have just missed something. I am drawing conclusions about you based on things in my past that didn't have anything to do with you!

Now let's look at another mode of thought:

Reflective mode
There is another mode of thought called reflective thinking. This is the most appropriate way to think when faced with situations where all the variables are not known (which is certainly any situation involving other people.) It is sometimes called receiver mode thinking because, unlike the memory mode where you actively go searching for answers in the mental database, reflective thinking is a process of allowing the answers to come to you.

Reflective thinking is like standing beside a flowing river watching ideas float by on the current. You notice them with interest, maybe even curiosity, but do not become attached to what you see. When you see something that looks good, you can pull it out.

The reflective mode is the realm of common sense. (Can you see that common sense is not directly tied to experience?) It is the realm of perspective where you suddenly see a bigger picture. It is also the realm of insight. When you spend most of your time in this mode, we call it wisdom.

I think you have experienced at least glimpses of this reflective mode of thinking. See if you can relate to this example:

Have you ever had a big problem, perhaps personal, perhaps professional, that you were working on? You strain your brain, thinking and thinking about what to do. You list pros and cons. You might become tense or irritable, your brow furrows, you have a hard time sleeping and still there is no answer in sight.

Then suddenly you have a insight – a real "whack in the head" experience – a blinding flash of the obvious where the perfect answer appears to you as if by magic! Has that ever happened to you? Probably.

Would I be safe to guess that the insight did not come in the middle of working on the problem? It may have come when you were just dropping off to sleep or just waking up. Perhaps in the shower, playing with the kids or puttering in the garden.

It might have appeared when you were on the golf course or relaxing on vacation. In short, it comes when your mind is quiet.

Reflective thinking is quiet-minded thought. When your mind quiets down, it automatically puts you in touch with a flow of deeper intelligence. This is where insights are found. Some call it women's intuition or a strong hunch. It is quietly watching ideas float by on the current and recognizing the ones that apply to the situation at hand.

Good and bad?
The two modes of thinking are not mutually exclusive. When your mind is quiet, you have instant access to anything stored in the database. If something in past experience is relevant, it will immediately occur to you. However, you do not go into a new situation burdened with old ideas that do not apply to the situation at hand.

You should also not infer that memory is bad and reflection is good – there is an appropriate place for each. Healthy psychological functioning, in fact, is defined as the appropriate use of both the memory and reflective modes of thinking.

Columbo management
Maintaining a quiet mind when dealing with another person is like being "dumb as dirt." You have no pre-conceived ideas about who they are, you make no judgements or assumptions about them, you do not automatically assume you know what they mean by what they say. You operate from a state of mild

puzzlement. It is a lot like Peter Falk's character in the TV series "Columbo."

When your mind is quiet and you are slightly puzzled, you tend to ask more probing questions – questions that will just naturally occur to you in the moment. You will be awash in fresh ideas.

Problems and conditions
I said earlier that a problem is only a situation where the solution has not yet occurred to you and that a condition is a situation that cannot be changed. How can you tell the difference? Just clear your mind, tap into that reflective mode of thinking and wait for the obvious answer to occur to you as an insight.

You will learn more, create a more positive climate and move your company farther when you deal with others from a quiet mind. In that state, you are not judgmental of others' ideas, your thoughts are fresh and you will see possibilities all around

Most people have had the experience of stumbling across quiet-minded insights, but the idea that you can actually function from there is a new one.

31
Lists

I know that you have a to-do list . . . and it is easy to think that working your list will move the company forward. Let's look at that idea next.

Think about what sort of thinking to-do lists typically represent – usually busy-minded thinking. ("I've got to do this, I've got to do that.")

Then think about what kind of thinking moves the company forward? Quiet-minded thinking, of course.

So how do you reconcile the two?

Let me share another story to illustrate. This one also involves my friend Mark Sneed of Phillips Seafood. In addition to four multi-million dollar restaurants, Mark is also responsible for Phillips' seafood plants around the world. He is a brilliant man who had increased his company's sales by over 60% in the last two years.

The other player in this short story is one of Mark's managers – also a skillful operator but also a man who is wedded to his to-do list. Give him a choice between his Day Timer and his left arm . . . and he will keep the book! He gets results, but always seems to be in a rush. Does that sound familiar?

Mark and I always give him a hard time about his list fixation but he still hasn't quite grasped what we are trying to help him see. A short while ago, we tried to make the point again. The three of us were having lunch and Mark was talking about how to make progress. He said, "Every once in awhile I have a list day. Yesterday was like that for me. There was a lot of things that I just had to do so I made my list and spent the day working on it."

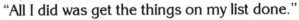

He said at the end of the day he had handled most of the things on his list. "But I didn't move the company anywhere yesterday," he said. "All I did was get the things on my list done."

"I move the company when I don't have a list, when my mind is quiet and I can see possibilities. I move the company when I can see things that we could be doing or where we might be creating a problem for ourselves." Think about it.

Where's the problem?
Lists in themselves are not the problem. Relying on lists can create a problem. Confusing activity with progress can be a problem. Thinking you are making progress because you did everything on your list can also mask a problem – maybe all you are doing is just spinning your wheels.

you can create a list out of a quiet mind. When you are struck with an insight, write it down, get quiet again and wait for another insight. Put these insights together and you will have a very powerful list.

There is even value in lists that come from a busy mind. In any business, there are always things that need to be done and getting them all down on a list can help keep your mind uncluttered. The key lies in what happens to them once they appear on the list.

Here are some better questions to ask yourself about your list:

Does this have to be done at all?

What would happen if this item was not addressed? You will be amazed at the number of things we do because we have always done them that wouldn't affect our business at all if they were not done.

Who is the best person to do this?

If it is something that has to be done, the next thing to determine is who the best person is to do it? It's back to the technique for solving problems again. Determine whose performance is most affected and whose behavior has to change and assign the task to them. Just because something initially appears on your list does not mean you are the one to do it.

Is this a high-return activity?

High-return activities are things you probably should do yourself. High-return activities include bringing in new business, organizing or energizing the staff or sponsoring charitable events – things that move the company forward.

Delegate low-return activities like scheduling, creating contests, ordering and inventories. Even most staff hiring is something that your crew can safely handle with a little coaching. (If you give people the opportunity, they will not hire jerks. After all, they will have to work with them!)

So much of what we take on is only because we have become attached to the idea that it is our job . . . then we wonder why we don't have any free time.

Every time you do a job that someone on your staff is capable of doing, you deprive them of an opportunity to learn. At the same time, you are not learning anything new, so nobody benefits.

All the day-to-day mechanics of running the place are activities that someone else on your staff can do or can learn how to do. Get busy. Get routine tasks off your plate. They only clutter up your mind and keep you from seeing possibilities that will move your company forward.

32
Stress

Do you feel stress as a normal part of being out there on the planet? Since stress on the job seems to be on the increase, it deserves a closer look.

We have funny ideas about stress. There is "stress management." Some people say a certain amount of stress is good for you. What insanity! Once you understand where stress really comes from, you can decide for yourself whether you want to stop it or not.

My favorite swamp philosopher, Pogo, put it very nicely when he said, "We have met the enemy and he is us." When it comes to stress, nobody is doing it to you except you. That may sound a little bit strange, so I will give you an analogy that I think may help. It is a golf analogy but you do not have to be a golfer to understand it.

A relaxing day of golf?
Let's say that it is a gorgeous day and you are going to play golf. You get up on the first tee, look down the fairway and think to yourself, "200 yards, just left of center." You line up the shot and whack that ball . . . 20 yards into the trees!

So you head down the fairway – 200 yards just left of center – to get the ball, because that is where it is "supposed" to be. When you get there, you look around for it. At first, you are a bit confused, then you get irritated and then you really get angry. You yell, "Where is my #@!% ball? It's supposed to be right here! Somebody's head is going to roll over this!" and throw a tantrum in the middle of the golf course because your ball is not where it is "supposed" to be. Basically a pretty stupid move!

It will not move the ball to that spot, the flow of the game stops, you look like a jerk and nobody wants to play with you anymore!

This is easy to see in golf – the ball is in the trees, go into the trees and play the ball! It's how you play the game.

Obvious in golf, perhaps, but how many times in your life have you done something that was "supposed" to produce a certain result, then gone to where that result was "supposed" to be and thrown a tantrum cause it was not there?

It will not produce the result, the flow of the game stops, you look like a jerk and nobody wants to play with you anymore!

When the game is on, the only option you have is to play the ball! The fact that you wanted the ball to be somewhere else is interesting, but has about as much relevance to the game as the color of your golf shirt!

This does not mean that you have to play out of the trees forever. When the game is over, take a lesson! When the game is over, see the golf pro for some advice on your swing . . . but when the game is on, you have no choice but to play the ball where it lies.

The root of stress
Here is where it gets interesting. Can you see that "200 yards just left of center" is just something you made up? Can you see that it is just a thought? You could have come up with something entirely different.

I call it a pre-determined idea. Pre-determined ideas are just your own thoughts . . . to which you become attached.

It is not a problem to stand on the first tee and think "200 yards just left of center" – it is only when you get attached to the thought that you will start to create difficulty for yourself.

Think about it. You made it up, you got attached to it and then you got angry when it didn't happen. Who is the villain here? Who is doing the thinking?

If you were not attached to where the ball went, you could shoot 300 and have a great day! But if you get it into your mind that you have to shoot an 80 or the day is a bust – and it's not happening – you get angry.

In the end, the ball is still going to get into the cup, it is just going to happen a little differently than the way you originally thought. Is this really a problem? Is it worth selling your peace of mind for?

The stress factors in our lives are just thoughts that we make up, then get attached to . . . and there are a lot of them:

"If you really cared, you would . . ."
"This shouldn't be happening . . ."
"It isn't right that . . ."
"We need more time to . . ."
"This all has to be done by . . ."
"You have no cause to . . ."

Who said so?

As in the golfing example, you had a thought, you got attached to it and then you got stressed out when it did not happen. The fact that you thought it up does not automatically make your idea true.

The only truth is that things are not playing out the way you made them up. Get over it. Once you can see that stress is really just a product of your own thinking, you have the power to do something about it.

Your level of stress goes down because you lose your tolerance for feeling stressed. As you spend more time with a quiet mind, it will feel like fingernails on the blackboard when your thinking gets speeded up and you start getting caught in your own thoughts of how things "should" be.

Whatever is happening in your life, accept it where it lies and play it from there – your stress will disappear and life will get much easier.

100

33
Warning signs

You can tell when you start to get caught in your own thinking because you will feel irritation, stress or even anger. You will find yourself thinking in terms of "should" and "should not," or "right" and "wrong." Your thoughts will become more negative and your body will tend to tighten up.

Learn to recognize the signs and take them for what they are – signals that you are starting to chase your tail. If you find yourself thinking ill of your kids, your mate, your staff or what's happening in your life, recognize that it's just a thought – another bubble from the bubble machine. It doesn't mean anything. Let it go and it will have no impact on you. Get attached to it and it will make your life miserable.

So when you sense a warning sign, the question to ask is, "Is the game on?" If the game is on, play the ball. If the game is over, take a lesson.

For example, if you are in the middle of the rush and discover you are out of a critical item, throwing a tantrum won't help. Play the ball – think, "How can I make this work without that item?" When the rush is over, take a lesson – look at how you ran out and see what you can do to keep it from happening again.

That's the way it works in business. That's the way it works in your life. Stress is a myth.

34
Pre-determined ideas

People, particularly people under pressure, have a tendency to resist anything that is at odds with their pre-determined idea (PDI) of how things "should be."

For example, let's say you are running a restaurant that offers a sandwich that includes french fries. In the middle of the rush, an elderly customer asks the server to substitute a small salad for the fries.

The server's first reaction may be to say "no" under any or all of the following conditions:

- if they take the request as an imposition (PDI: customers should not deliberately try to make my day more complicated)

- if the substitution will mean more work to place the order (PDI: customers should understand that I don't have time for this right now)

- if they don't know how to enter the substitution in the computerized ordering system (PDI: customers should not try to confuse me when I am busy)

- if they think that the patron is just being contrary (PDI: customers should be happy with what is offered on the menu).

- if they think that everyone must be treated the same way (PDI: if I let one person do it, I will have to let everyone do it)

If you had a staff member who behaved in this way – who habitually said "no" as a knee-jerk reaction – you might conclude that they "had an attitude" or were not service-oriented. After all, if they cannot easily see what is required to accommodate the customer's request, or if they are not willing to consider a new idea and try to handle it, they should not be working in a service industry, right?

Where did they ever get such a negative outlook? You would certainly never do anything like that . . . or would you?

In the interests of introspection, let's say you are in the middle of the managerial juggling act (trying to keep sales up, keep costs down, find good staff, put out fires, have a life and the like) and one of your staff makes a last-minute request for a schedule change.

Your first reaction might well be to say "no" under any or all of the following conditions:

- if you take the request as an imposition (PDI: employees should not deliberately try to make my day more complicated)

- if the substitution will mean more work to rearrange the schedule (PDI: employees should understand I don't have time for this right now)

- if you don't know how you are going to be able to accommodate the change (PDI: employees should not try to confuse me when I am busy)

- if you think that the staff member is being contrary (PDI: employees should be happy with the schedule the way it was originally written)

- if you think that everyone must be treated the same way (PDI: if I let one person do it, I will have to let everyone do it)

Do you see what I mean? This is just an illustration of how easily we can get caught in our own thinking and how it reflects in the behavior of our staff.

How it "should be"

In both these examples, the problem grows out of a pre-determined idea – something that one person has decided in advance **should** go a certain way. We all do this and there is no fault in merely having the thought. The difficulty comes when you become attached to your idea of how things **should** be.

Your idea of how things "should" be is only a thought that you had. Somebody told you something and you believed them or you just got an idea in your head. Who said that the information was true? When you give thoughts more legitimacy than they deserve, you can get yourself in a lot of trouble.

Role models

So what does all this have to do with life in the real world of business? As a start, it may help you make course corrections with your staff.

For example, if your crew seems focused on what they **cannot** do for your customers (as opposed to thinking about what they **can** do), make very sure you are not, in fact, guilty of exactly the same behavior.

Interestingly, getting the staff to say "yes" starts with the attitude and actions of management. What **they** see is what **you** will get.

Do you roll your eyes and think, "what a jerk" when someone on your staff behaves in a certain way? Your behavior toward your crew in the daily course of business provides the model for how your staff will behave when one of your patrons makes a "weird request" or does something they weren't "supposed" to have done.

As a start, see how often you can have phrases like these be the first words from your lips, particularly when something unexpected comes up:

"Of course we can!"
"It would be my pleasure."
"It will be no problem at all."
"I never thought of that."
"What an interesting idea!"

Keep in mind that you are the role model . . . whether you want the job or not!

35
Start to notice

Start to notice your own tendency to resist anything that is at odds with **your** pre-determined ideas of how things are "supposed to be."

Lighten up
Start to notice when you think "that's wrong" any time a staff member shows initiative and does something differently from the way you would have done it.

Watch yourself
Start to notice your reaction when a staff member asks you for something outside the normal routine of things, like a last-minute schedule change. Again, you are the role model.

Relax
Start to notice any thought that contains a "should" or a "supposed to" and be wary of it. When your brain bubbles up a "should" idea, just let it pass. Do not allow yourself to take it seriously or get attached to it. It is only a thought and it has no importance other than what you arbitrarily choose to assign it.

Listen

Start to notice what happens when you are not listening to what other people *mean* by what they say. You (and they) can tell when you are not listening because you will have an answer in your mind before they even stop talking. Do not presume that your experiences have relevance to another person.

Learn

Start to notice that other people's actions and requests make sense to them. The fact that they may or may not make sense to you is not required.

Open up

Start to notice what happens if you allow yourself more than a passing thought that things "should not" be happening the way they are happening. Notice how just the thought can paralyze you and how judgmental the thought is. Notice how disrespectful, indifferent and impersonal you seem to others when you think your view of the world is better than theirs.

Wake up

Start to notice when your own agenda seems more important than that of the people you are dealing with, be they customers, staff or family. Notice how unserved those people feel when it happens.

In short, notice your pre-determined ideas and don't let them run your life. We all have our personal preferences, but attempting to impose your view of the world – your pre-determined ideas – on others is disrespectful. It will only preserve the status quo and keep you from seeing fresh possibilities.

36
Don't compete

Nearly every market is experiencing a major influx of new business and it doesn't matter if they are national operations with deep pockets and smooth formats or independents trying to carve out a niche or pursue a dream.

In either case, many managers seem to spend more and more time worrying about competitors, looking over their shoulders, counting cars and trying to outguess the new guys.

When they ask me what they should do, I tell them to stop trying to compete – that competing can be dangerous to their professional survival!

Let me explain with an example:

Have you ever been driving down the road and had a police car following you? I don't know about you but when that happens to me, I suddenly become fixated on the speedometer and fascinated by my rear view mirror!

In this condition, I have a lot less energy available to focus on where I am going! The closer an eye I keep on the cop, the higher my anxiety level rises and I am prone to making more silly mistakes. I am definitely not as good a driver when I am paying too much attention to who or what is behind me!

The same thing applies in the business world. When you are watching the competition, it drains vital energy away from your primary focus which should be on making sure you run the very best business you can.

An obsession with your competitors can cause you to make silly mistakes. Paying too much attention to what others are doing can interfere with giving your customers a consistently memorable time!

Wake up!

Be competitive . . . but don't compete. Know what your major competitors are doing but don't become obsessive about it. You cannot prosper by doing what they are doing – you can only thrive by doing what *you* do better than anyone else can do it.

Monetary success and personal joy will come when your sole concern – your driving passion – is only how you can excel!

37
Tone of voice

A final insight into dealing with people is this: the message you send is not communicated by your choice of words. In fact, the message you deliver is always contained in the *feeling* behind the tone of voice you use.

Your words, while important, are only a vehicle that carries the emphasis, inflections and feelings bearing the message that others receive.

You can probably recall a recent incident in which someone said one thing to you but conveyed a totally different message by the way that they said it. Which message did you believe?

Everyone makes assumptions, forms judgments and draws conclusions from another's tone of voice. If you have ever watched a foreign language film or been in a country where you did not speak the language, you probably still had a pretty good sense of what was happening, even if you could not discern all the details.

The typical manager's day can be hectic. As the pace picks up, it is easy to forget the importance of voice tone when dealing with others. Under pressure you can easily snap off a fast answer or react in a way that delivers a message entirely different from the one made up of your words.

If you talk to people in a disrespectful tone, more often than not you will get a negative reaction. If you speak in a pleading tone, people will not take you seriously. Either extreme hampers productivity.

However, a neutral tone will automatically foster an adult relationship between you and your staff which will improve the work climate. In a higher climate, your staff is naturally inclined to provide exceptional service to your customers, feel more involved in their work and identify more closely with the company.

To help make sure your intonation matches your intention when you are talking with someone, pause before speaking, clear your head of any distracting thoughts and allow yourself to connect with the other person. Then simply say what you need to say.

Good communication starts with cleaning up your internal state – a process that is quite natural. When you start becoming aware of your distractions, you will automatically start the process of self-correction.

You will be surprised and pleased by how clear your communication will become, how infrequently little misunderstandings will arise and how effective you will become at human relations.

Part 4

Yeah, but . . .

38
Getting acclimated

When the common sense of this approach first struck me and I finally saw a way out of my world of weeds, I did not know for sure if it was even possible to run a business the way I am suggesting in this book. After all, I had spent my entire career to that point getting quite good at forcing things to happen.

What I *was* certain of, however, was that kicking butt, taking names and working 80 + hours a week was no longer my idea of a good time.

Once I saw it, this new vision was the only approach that made sense to me. I figured if I couldn't run a restaurant this way, I would sell auto parts! My peace of mind had become more important to me than my ability to work myself into an early grave.

What I wasn't prepared for was how effective it was. I honestly put in half the time I had ever applied to a job in my life . . . and honestly got twice as much accomplished as I ever had in my life. If I had been willing to work less, I could have gotten more done! Go figure!

However, I had some questions as I started down this new road and I suspect you may have a few as well. In the next few chapters, I will address several of the more common areas that people seem to have trouble grasping as they shift to a new understanding.

39
Out to lunch

You may have gathered that when you are having a bad day, that is a great time to disappear into the office and do paperwork rather than wander around and bring down the mood of the entire operation.

However, there are only so many times you can tell the boss, "Well, I felt a little off track so I went out to play golf." He may suggest you look for a new job at the golf club!

So what do you do when you are a little "out to lunch" and still have to perform? Here are a few suggestions that may help:

Can you live with it?
When you are a little lost, the tendency is to feel that you must take action RIGHT NOW. Do you really have to do something immediately . . . or could it wait until you are seeing things more clearly? If so, put it off.

Recognize your state of mind

If you cannot delay action until a better time, the best thing you can do is to realize that you are a little "out to lunch" and are not seeing things quire clearly. Do not trust your perceptions – everything looks like a disaster when you are in a bad mood.

Listen

The fastest way to regain your perspective and innate wisdom is to quiet your mind, realize that you don't have a clue . . . and listen. Listen with humility. Listen with curiosity, Listen for an insight.

Trust the process

When the insight strikes you, just follow that idea and it will bring you right back into balance every time.

A case study

Let me share a story of how this process worked for me. I had an employee, Darryl, who was a real rising star for me. He was coming on strong and I had big plans for Darryl.

But suddenly he started to self-destruct, doing things that were just way out of character. For example, we had slick floors, so we had issued non-slip shoes to all our workers. Darryl came to work in the middle of the Colorado winter wearing his leather sole dress shoes, slipped and had a Worker's Comp claim.

I didn't know what was going on, but I knew that I couldn't live with it any longer, so I caught him on a break one day and said, "Darryl, I don't have a clue as to what is going on here." (And I didn't. I didn't even know what I was going to say after I said that!)

117

My mind quieted down and suddenly I had an idea that had never occurred to me before – I just went with it. "But if I had to guess," I went on, "my guess would be that you really want to get out of this job, but you just can't quite figure out how to do it."

Darryl got a little smile on his face and said, "Well you know, you're pretty close." I was curious and said, "What do you want to do?" and he replied, "I think I'd better get out of here."

Contrast this approach to the way you might normally be tempted to deal with a situation like this: ("What's your problem? You are better than this, Darryl!")

It is shocking how often we can be so certain about things when we have no real clue about what is really happening.

I will grant you that there is a certain leap of faith in handling things in this manner, but if you don't have a clue, there is no use pretending that you do – just quiet your mind and trust that the answer will appear.

It will . . . and it will be right on the money every time!

40
Non-compliance

Let's say that you want a member of your staff to achieve a certain result and it is just not happening.

The old model of management would call for several counseling sessions (all properly documented, of course) followed by termination if the person was unable to deliver the needed results.

While termination may sometimes be an appropriate course of action, are there any other possibilities that might explain a lack of performance and help salvage the situation?

Here are a few potential explanations for the lapse in achievement I suggest you explore – and roughly in the order listed – before you decide to cut a marginal employee loose:

They don't understand what you want

Just because you know the results you are trying to achieve doesn't mean that your staff automatically does, so the first step is to be very certain they know exactly what you are after.

This is not as easy as it sounds. Lee Cockrell, VP of Walt Disney World once told me that people cannot deliver a higher level of customer service than they have personally experienced. If what he says is true (and I believe it is), does it make any sense to fire a person for delivering poor service when they really have no clear idea what you are talking about?

So the first thing to determine is whether or not the employee has a true grasp of what you are asking and that you are not expecting something that is beyond their comprehension, even if (especially if) it seems obvious to you.

They don't understand why it is important

If, after really listening to the person, you are certain that they know what you want, the next possibility is that they don't understand why it is important.

In the foodservice industry, sanitation practices can easily fall into this category. Based on experience, I would say that many workers, both in service and retail operations, apparently have no understanding of the value of a repeat customer.

Whose fault is that? If we do not tell them, how are they supposed to know? So the next step in resolving performance issues is to educate the staff member on the importance of what you are requesting.

They don't understand how to do it

Particularly if you have a tendency to yell at someone when they make a mistake, your staff will never tell you that they don't know how to do something you ask. Nobody likes to be yelled at. They will just smile, nod their heads and hope you will go away.

The mystery of the mop

I can give you an example from personal experience: At the age of 14, I was hired by a small restaurant on Cape Cod for my first job – washing dishes (by hand!) during the summer tourist season. The training for my frightening new responsibilities was concise and pointed – a single sentence: "Get back there and do it!" This was followed by one sentence of counseling: "If you screw up, you're out of here!" Ah, the world of work!

Like most teenagers in the old days before automatic dishwashers, I had *lots* of dishwashing experience, so that part of the job was pretty easy. But I still remember my terror the first time I was pointed in the general direction of the cleaning gear and told to mop the floor.

Talk about panic! I'd never seen a string mop in my life! We certainly didn't use one at home so I had no idea what it was or how to use it. My boss had me so terrified of making a mistake that I didn't dare reveal my ignorance by asking him to show me what to do. After all, if I screwed up, I would be fired!

Fortunately, Manny, one of the breakfast cooks, saw the terror in my eyes and took me under his wing. He realized I was clueless, taught me how to use the mop and patiently worked with me until I had mastered it.

In addition to being my mentor, he also became my inspector, making me re-do anything that didn't meet his standards while making sure I understood why it was important to do it a certain way.

Almost single-handedly, Manny helped me survive my first big adventure in employment. Thinking back on the experience, it is interesting to realize that I still remember Manny, but the names of the boss and the restaurant have long since slipped from my memory.

121

The lesson here is that just because *you* know how to do something does not mean that everybody else on the planet does. You would do well to ascertain the facts before taking more radical action.

It doesn't have to be done!
If things are still not happening, another explanation could be that it really doesn't make any difference in the daily operation whether it is done or not!

Admittedly, this is seldom the case, but too often we do things just "because we have always done them." At the OTC, I eliminated two days of counting, pricing and extending food inventories once I learned that nobody ever did anything with the figures!

They have a better way to do it
If the task needs to be done and the what, why and how are covered, the next possibility is they are not doing it your way because they have a better way to do it!

(This might be a good time to re-read the discussion about the value of lazy people on Page 86.)

The way to avoid this trap is to focus on results rather than activities. If you are getting the results you want and no laws are being broken, who cares if one of your workers does it differently than the way you would?

When you define results rather than activities, you allow people to interpret their jobs in a way that works for them and that will always improve both retention and productivity.

They can't do it
The next possibility is that they just can't do what you want – physically or mentally it is simply beyond their capabilities. This does not make them incompetent, it just means they are mis-cast.

If you put a "numbers person" in a customer contact position or place a "people person" in a job where they have no interaction with others, you are likely to see performance problems. As in the example of Chris the dishwasher, just because someone is not good at one job doesn't mean they couldn't be excellent in another.

They won't do it

If you are comfortable that all the possibilities above have been considered, and you are still not getting the performance you need, the only other explanation is that the person just will not do what you need done.

In that case, do yourself and the employee a favor and "free up their future" to pursue another line of work! Everybody is good at something but not everybody is good at what you need done.

Given how difficult it is to find and retain quality staff, termination should be the option of last choice. Do not give up on anyone until you have given them every opportunity to succeed.

41

Freeing up the future

Shortly after I started working with these new ideas, I had a problem: a member of my staff who was not performing up to my standards. If I could have become angry, I could have fired her, but I saw that she was doing the best she could. Still, I was not getting the performance I needed. I knew I had to do something . . . but what?

The operable question is, "can you live with it?" If you can, keep coaching. If you can't, do what you have to do. Here is my approach to letting someone go.

How bad can you get?
By way of background, I must confess that I was never very good at firing people. How bad? When I was running a hotel in the Virgin Islands, I let one of my staff go and did it so poorly that the entire crew walked out in protest and someone came back in the middle of the night and sabotaged the water system in the condos. That is bad! (In self-defense, I should point out that I was working 120 hours a week and was totally brain dead, but that is no excuse.)

In contrast, if I fired twenty people in the course of my 4½ years at the Olympics – and I probably did – nineteen of them thanked me! I was stunned!

Based on my application of the principles we have discussed, here is my format for letting someone go:

Can you live with it?
If you can, keep coaching. The question is less about whether they **can** do the job than it is about whether they **will** do the job. This is the time for you to explore the possibilities we discussed in the previous chapter.

Respect the power of timing
If you can't live with it, pick your moment as best you can. Understand that there is a time when people can hear you and there is a time when they can't. If you have just had a major upset on the job, this is not the time to have a serious discussion about someone's future with the company. Take a break and deal with it when everyone is in a more receptive mood.

Maintain a no-fault perspective
Understand that is not their fault. They asked for a job and you gave it to them. We all tried our best but it just didn't work. You do not need a "bad guy" and, in fact, looking for one will only make things worse.

Operate from respect
Just because someone did not meet your performance standards does not make them a bad person. They are good at something but this just wasn't it! Respect is a key factor in keeping the exchange on a positive level.

Be clear and direct
Don't beat around the bush. Get to the point quickly

and say what you have to say. It will be less painful (and more respectful) for everyone involved.

Clean it up and move on
If you make a mess, take responsibility for cleaning it up and get on with your life. All you can do is the best you can do and it won't necessarily go smoothly every time.

Adios, Harry
To illustrate, let's say that is time to let Harry go. You have worked with him and worked with him and it is just not happening. Pick your moment as best you can and when Harry comes into the office, the scene might sound roughly like this:

> *"Harry, this just isn't working. You know it and I know it . . . and it is frustrating to me. I am sure that if I was more skillful, we might have found a way to make it work, but I have tried everything I can think of . . . and I know you have, too.*
>
> *There are just too many other demands on my time and I can't spend any more time on this. You are going to have to find something else."*

It doesn't have to be any more complicated than this. The fact that it isn't working should not come as a surprise to anyone and you won't do Harry (or yourself) any favors by dragging out the inevitable.

42

Reaching agreement

You will find that life will get easier as you apply these principles to your daily routine. Becoming a better listener and being open to the ideas of your staff will take you into exciting new realms, but I am not advocating management by committee.

The final call and ultimate responsibility still lies with management and realistically, you will not always be in complete agreement with your staff on everything. Still, you need to proceed as smoothly as possible, so here are a few suggestions on reaching a relatively painless agreement when you find yourself at odds:

Establish a climate for a meeting of the minds
The first step in reaching agreement is be sure you are setting yourself up to succeed. Here are the items to consider as you get started:

Respect the power of timing
Pick your moment. You want to find a time when the group is not distracted by business pressure and can focus on the task at hand without distractions.

Recognize the power of a supportive atmosphere
Rapport is the lubricant of agreement – don't leave

home without it! If the group cannot reach a point of feeling comfortable together you will never reach a meaningful accord, so take the time to "plug in" with each other before proceeding.

At first glance, this may seem like wasting time to those who want to "get on with it," but in the long run it will greatly shorten the time to come to a true meeting of the minds.

Listen for insights

Do you notice how often thoughtful listening is a key management skill? You want to listen for the content, of course, but it is also important to listen for insight and understanding. The other person's position makes sense to them and it will help you to understand why before you proceed.

Until the other parties feel that you "get" what they are saying, they will be fixated on getting you to see their point of view. You do not even need to agree, disagree or express an opinion, just understand why they see things the way they do.

When you listen for insights, you do not really know *what* you are listening for . . . but you will recognize it when you hear it.

Work from agreement

Once you have established a strong connection, the next step is to start establishing agreement. Each point you can agree on will deepen the connection and raise the climate in the group. As the climate improves, items that once looked contentious take on less significance and agreement will become easier.

Agree on the things you can agree on

There may be a number of things you can agree on at the outset. These might include the goals you

128

have in this situation (to find a solution that will produce a certain result) or your intention in the negotiation (everybody will be able to feel good about what we finally decide to do).

You may be able to easily agree on the financial considerations that may be at play (we have X dollars in the budget or we must leave enough cash reserves to meet unexpected needs).

There may be operational considerations (we must be sure the smooth flow of service to the patron is not interrupted). Perhaps all parties can agree on the time frame for implementing a solution.

What you agree on at this point is less critical than the fact that you start agreeing on *something.* The climate will improve with each point of agreement which, in turn, makes further harmony more likely.

Defer points of contention

When you run into an area where you cannot agree easily, don't dwell on it. "I can see we need to talk about this in more detail. Let's make a note and come back to it later."

Keep in mind that agreement will raise the climate (and the likelihood of success) and disagreement will lower it. Keep the tone positive.

Clean up the details

Once you've agreed on everything you can, go back over the list of unresolved items. You may find some that appeared to be sticking points earlier no longer look that way. You can tick them off the list, leaving fewer and fewer issues to be resolved.

Agree on relative priorities

Always moving toward what you can agree on, you may be able to agree that one point is more critical than another ("If it means staying within the budget, we can take a little longer to do it.) This will put more items into the "completed" pile and make the task look easier and easier.

Dialogue on any unresolved points
Now you are down to the core issues and it is time for a true dialogue – the free-flowing exchange of ideas. It calls for reflective listening and a sincere willingness to change your position.

This is the time to realize that reaching a workable solution is ultimately more important than exactly what that solution looks like. Give up the need to be right in favor of having the company win.

Give this part of the process as much time as the particular problem deserves. It will take you longer to reach agreement than if you made an executive decision, but the time it will take to implement the solution will be substantially shorter. Consensus will also have a more positive effect on the climate and working environment in the company.

Agree on how you will measure progress
It is easy to overlook this point, but it is important to reach consensus on how you will monitor progress to assure that the agreement you reach is working and what you will do if things start to get off track.

Be part of the solution
As a final point, take personal responsibility for the success of the process. You are the role model here as well and others will follow your example.

Be an advocate for others
Look for ways that you can help them get what they want from the final resolution.

Be certain, not stubborn

You may have certain non-negotiable standards that figure into the situation but be aware that you can hold to them without being a jerk or making anyone wrong.

Certainty in action

Since this is an important point, permit me a brief story to illustrate: I tend to drive a little fast and in twelve years of living in California, I had occasion to run into the California Highway Patrol once or twice. Their officers are extremely courteous, personable and respectful . . . and there is never one flicker of doubt but that you are going to get a ticket!

Because the thought of talking your way out of it is not even a possibility in the officer's consciousness, it does not even cross your mind to attempt it! That is what I mean by certainty.

In my own case, I am certain that you cannot work for me and steal from me, use drugs or have poor sanitation practices. These are like gravity to me.

Because I was certain about these points and did not even have a thought in my head that they were negotiable, my staff did not argue them with me. I would not disrespect other ideas or fail to listen to differing opinions if they were offered, but I was not inclined to compromise in these areas.

Set a personal example

As a final point, always conduct yourself as you would want the others in the group to conduct themselves. Listen. Reflect. Be flexible where you can. Ask good questions. Listen and reflect some more. What they see is what you will get.

Disagreements can often be a catalyst for meaningful changes in your organization. Embrace them when they appear, handle them with skill and respect. You and your company will be better for the experience.

Part 5

Where To From Here?

43
The daily question

What did you learn from your staff today?

I often pose this question to operators in my seminars and it is worth bringing up again. It is a reminder that if you don't have a fresh answer to this question every day, then you are not listening.

If you are not listening, you are not learning. If you are not learning, you are not growing. If you are not growing, you are dead!

I recently asked this question of the people who attended one of my seminars and received the following replies that might offer a few insights.

I had this exchange with Grant Webb who owns East Side Mario's in Ottawa, Canada:

I learned several things:

1) One of my newer but weaker staff is great at suggesting side salads as an add-on at lunch time. I gave her a pat on the back and told her to keep up the good work.

2) I asked my bartender how things were going.

She said many of the staff were not following opening and closing duty lists on the patio and she finds this very frustrating. I told her I understood and that I appreciated her feedback.

I will ask some of the other staff the same question in the next few days. I have a feeling that if I ask if they feel the duties were being done right or not, the work will improve on its own – just due to my interest. The best thing is, no discipline is needed to make this happen.

3) I found out a new dishwasher I have teaches developmentally challenged kids how to skate.

4) I asked one of my servers why she was a little off and learned she was very hung over. I thanked her for doing her best and asked if she felt a little silly for punishing herself and her guests with inferior service.

5) I had a chat with another staff member about gardening and kid's camps (she has two children). I told her I'd bring some info about a camp I was enrolling my son in.

Thanks for the reminder. I will try to learn more tomorrow.

I responded:

Great news! Amazing what you can learn if you listen. Amazing what you can get done when you don't try to do it all!

Grant wrote back:

It is amazing what you can learn when you really listen and it is also amazing what you can see *when you actually "watch." We often find ourselves caught up in the dynamics of this business and forget what our true roles are.*

*My partner Roy and I used to kid each other that we were the highest paid busboys in the city! Not that there is anything wrong in helping out when you are truly needed. The trick is **not** helping out when you are **not** needed. This is something I always knew, but now am finally putting in to practice.*

I think my staff appreciates my feedback and communication more than my running food for them – especially when they don't need it!

I also heard from Scott Bogart, a CPA in the LA area who does CFO work for a variety of clients. He wrote:

I really enjoyed your class. Even though your program was designed for the restaurant industry, at least 90% is applicable to ALL BUSINESSES. I am applying the ideas to all my restaurant and non-restaurant clients.

For one of my non-restaurant clients, I was retained to come in and do CFO work. As it usually happens, I ended up becoming involved in issues that go well beyond the financial arena. A recent issue involved terminating a Vice President who showed little interest or respect for the thoughts and ideas of her subordinates.

Part of the transition has involved listening to the opinions and creative ideas of the staff she left behind, a staff that up until her departure was sending out resumes because they didn't like coming to work any more.

Before we decided to let her go, we were concerned about the void and how things were going to get done. By moving her out of the way and engaging her staff in dialogue about the tasks at hand, they got excited about coming to work again.

The challenges don't seem very big anymore. It seems like the sun came out and everyone jumped "above the line."

My point is that you can tap this incredible source of information just by seeing its value. You do not have to have the answers, you just need to be able to find them . . . and one of the most potent things you can do is to listen – really listen – to your staff.

If you listen you will learn. You might learn something you didn't know. You might get an insight into how another person sees the world. You might pick up an idea that leads to entirely new growth opportunities.

But first you have to quiet your mind and really listen. At the very least, sit down with each member of your staff one-on-one and find out who they really are, what they want to be when they grow up and what ideas they have to make your company better.

What did **you** learn from **your** staff today?

44

Fix the system, not the people

There is always something to handle in the world of business and it can drive you crazy! I know managers who continually moan that "you just can't find good people anymore" or "these kids today just don't want to work." What rubbish!

The only problem here is the way these managers are looking at the problems. When dealing with daily operating issues, I urge you to look for failures in the system, not for failures in people.

Where's my meal?
Here is another restaurant example that will illustrate what I mean: Let's say that you have a standard that calls for food orders to be on the table within fifteen minutes of the time they are placed.

> **Note:** You determined this standard by observing when the majority of your guests start to become aware of the slow pace of service. By one means or another you have discovered that a ticket time of 15 minutes is what it takes in your operation to meet your guests' needs and expectations during this meal period. I suspect other businesses have similar sorts of standards that are a measure of their success.

Let's also say that Scott in the pantry notices that orders often take 20 minutes to get out of his station. Scott is aware you want the food out in 15 minutes so he has two options:

1. He can come to you and report the delays.
2. He can keep quiet, hoping you won't notice

If you see the failure as a result of Scott's poor job performance, you will blame Scott when you learn of the excessive processing times. ("Thanks for telling me that, Scott. There's obviously a problem here and it's *you!* Since you can't meet our standards, you're fired.") If Scott suspects this will be your reaction, he will never open his mouth! Don't laugh. Variations on this scene happen all the time.

People failures

If you see operating problems as people failures, you virtually guarantee that no one on your staff will ever tell you when things break down. In such a working environment, not many folks will "rat" on their co-workers – they will figure it is management's job to know what's going on and will not want to feel they are responsible for someone else losing their job.

Certainly no one will report a problem that is a result of their own inability to perform if making that report is likely to be professional suicide!

The predictable results: customer service suffers, operating problems are perpetuated, the "them and us" attitude is strengthened and your conscientious workers are more likely to become disenchanted. All of this will eventually show up as reduced sales volume, lower morale and increased turnover.

140

System failures
If you see operational breakdowns as failures in the *system*, you will greet Scott's report with enthusiasm and gratitude – enthusiasm because he is taking responsibility for the success of the operation and gratitude because he provided an insight into where you were failing to deliver the desired level of service.

You might then sit down with Scott to explore where the system might be weak and see what suggestions he has on how to change the system to fix or eliminate the problems.

Look to the system
There are a number of possible breakdowns in the system that could account for the slow ticket times:

- Perhaps the menu is heavy on pantry items and the station is overloaded.

- Maybe there is an item so complicated to prepare that every time someone orders it, the entire production flow jams up.

- Perhaps necessary supplies are kept in an inconvenient place and production slows down when a particular item is ordered.

- Perhaps there is a needed piece of equipment that is missing or malfunctioning.

- Perhaps Scott does not know how to operate the necessary equipment.

- Perhaps orders are garbled when they come in from the dining room because the service staff doesn't understand how to use the new computer system. Every time and order is not clear, it might take a lot of additional discussion with the service staff to sort it out and get it right.

141

- Perhaps Scott can't read and has been trying to keep you from finding out.

Even if the problem is a result of Scott's inability to perform, it is still a system failure:

- If Scott was not properly trained, if he does not understand what you want him to do or does not grasp why it is important, you have a breakdown in your training and supervisory systems.

- If the performance standard itself is unreasonable given the labor you have scheduled, you have a breakdown in the staffing system or you may need to reconsider your means of setting standards.

- If Scott is not physically or mentally capable of doing what the position demands or if Scott is otherwise the wrong person for that particular job, he may be more productive in another position. You need to look for where the job assignment system broke down in allowing him to be assigned to the pantry in the first place.

- If Scott is the wrong sort of person to be working in your business at all, there is a problem in your staff selection system that allowed him to be hired.

But the problem is always in the system, never in the people.

45
Making it safe

When you look for failures in the system and not for failures in people, it makes it safe for your existing staff to tell you where the snags are.

They are the people most likely to know what is not working properly. Getting your crew involved means that the burden of keeping the train on the tracks does not fall entirely on management. That in itself can be a great relief!

While it is easy (and tempting) to blame individuals for operational problems, it is never productive. The problem is not with your people. All they did was ask for a job – *you* are the one that gave it to them!

This is not about pointing fingers or assigning blame. If you regard any lapses as *your* responsibility, you can do something about them. If the problems are always someone else's fault, you will only continue to be frustrated, spin your wheels and perpetuate the same old headaches.

Making the shift
So how can you move your organization to a point where people feel free to open up?

If you have been a control-oriented manager who has always assigned blame and tried to keep your staff firmly under your thumb, it is going to take some time to regain their trust and confidence. It will be difficult but it can be done.

For managers to do their jobs properly, they do not need to *have* all the right answers, they simply must be able to *find* the right answers.

Here are some management qualities that will help you establish this dialogue with your staff and start to change things for the better:

Listen to your staff

Listen to more than just to what they say. Listen with curiosity. Listen with humility. Listen for the feelings behind the words. Listen for insights. If you are willing to put your own judgements and opinions on hold and be "dumb as dirt," it will help you keep an open mind and help your staff feel better-heard. You might learn something as well!

Consider what they have to say

They are closer to most problems than you are and they have a different perspective on what is happening. Their observations are as valid for them as yours are for you. There is wisdom and insight in your staff if you are courageous enough to place a higher value on preserving your business than on protecting your ego.

144

Acknowledge their contributions

What gets rewarded is what gets done. I encourage you to consider some sort of reward to acknowledge how much you value reports of failures in the system. In my experience, people are eager to become part of the solution when they get rewarded (with gratitude if nothing else) for identifying areas that could be working better.

Act on what they tell you

Nothing validates people's opinions like taking action on their ideas. This is not to suggest that every idea will be a "keeper," but do not pass up a good idea just because you did not think of it first. If people see that something actually happens when they share their ideas and observations, they gain hope, the "them and us" distinction starts to fade and most will take extra care to suggest only ideas they know will actually make things better.

By eagerly seeking out breakdowns in the system and sincerely welcoming information that shows where the company is falling short of its goals or failing to meet its standards, you make it possible for your crew to become part of the solution.

Tapping the talent available in your staff will make it easier to spot the real causes of your problems. Better yet, it will be easier to identify how you might change things to make your problems disappear!

46
Dumb as dirt

We all like to think of ourselves as smart people . . . or at least nobody wants to think of themself as dumb. Let's take a look at each of these possibilities as it relates to dealing with your staff.

"Smart" people
Smart people always figure they have the best answer to a given situation. When a "smart" person solicits someone else's opinion, all the time knowing that they already have the "best" answer, they don't listen.

Did you ever deal with a person like this? What did you think of them? My guess is that they came across as a jerk and looked really stupid to you!

"Dumb" people
In contrast, when you solicit someone else's opinion and you have no preconceived idea of what you want to hear, it forces you to really listen closely to everything they say.

From your perspective, you may feel rather dumb, but to the person you are dealing with – whose ideas have just been thoroughly considered – you look very smart, indeed. It is just quiet-minded listening.

A quiet mind is very powerful when dealing with other people. (It is interesting that the less you know, the smarter you look to others . . . and the less you know, the more you learn!)

A truly smart person realizes that there is a wealth of information available outside of themself and seeks to tap into it.

Remember that everything you already know is what got you into the situations you are in. The only thing that will move you ahead is information that you don't yet have – and that will only come from listening to new sources and gaining new insights.

Since it is stupid to stay stuck and smart to move ahead . . . you figure it out!

47
A meeting of the minds

When was the last time you held a really world class staff meeting – a gathering that was so productive and enjoyable that people left more energized than when they arrived! Did you even realize that such a meeting was possible?

If the idea of a truly invigorating staff meeting seems foreign to your experience, you are not alone. The sad fact is that most staff meetings . . . aren't! In practice, most meetings of the staff are typically little more than management sermons.

Worse yet, they are often presented in a distracted, condescending manner that causes the crew to roll their eyes, shut down their brains and experience a drop in energy. No wonder everybody dreads them!

A truly effective staff meeting is more about reaching a meeting of the minds than simply accomplishing a gathering of bodies and the old models don't work.

However, if you take a different approach, your staff meetings can help you head off most emergencies before they arise, reduce problems that require your attention, lower your staff turnover and help create a smoother-running, more profitable operation.

For the purposes of this section, I am talking about pre-shift meetings as distinguished from more formal sessions devoted exclusively to skill training. These are fairly common in the hospitality industry and they deserve a place in any service-oriented business.

At any rate, forget everything you ever knew about staff meetings and let's take a fresh look:

The primary objective of staff meetings is to create a positive feeling in the group.

A positive feeling helps people naturally recognize what they have in common. When the feeling in the group is warm and supportive, it is easier to see that everyone is in it together and that the success of each individual is inseparable from the success of the entire group.

Without a good feeling, people tend to stay focused on their differences. This close feeling is more likely to result from an appreciative sharing of the good news – and there is usually quite a bit when you make a point of looking for it.

Staff meetings are not the time to address individual shortcomings – that should be done one-on-one in private – and they are certainly not an appropriate time to dwell on group failings.

The second objective is to open a dialogue.

A dialogue is a comfortable two-way flow of ideas that leaves all the participants feeling connected and important. With this sort of rapport, your meetings naturally tend to instill understanding rather than simply passing along knowledge.

149

The difference is significant because understanding "sticks" where information is soon forgotten. In addition, the flow of ideas back to management helps eliminate the "them and us" mentality and helps your staff feel that it is also *their* company.

By bringing your staff into the loop, soliciting, considering and valuing their ideas, staff meetings can help establish and enhance the feeling of teamwork in the operation. This is likely to result in improved customer service, productivity and profitability.

The third objective of staff meetings is training.

A properly conducted staff meeting is a forum for continuous improvement. Even if you have a training program, never miss a chance to pass along a few more hints. This is a perfect opportunity to do it.

If you don't train, you deliver one of two messages: either people are delivering exactly the results you want and can't possibly get any better or that any ninny can instinctively be successful without training. I doubt that either case is true.

48
Mindset

When you decide to get serious about staff meetings, it is critical to commit to holding them on a regular basis – ideally before every shift every day – no matter what is going on that day.

When meetings are sporadic or frequently canceled because of other pressures (and there are **always** other pressures), it shows the importance you give these meetings. If staff meetings are not important to you, they will certainly not be important to your crew.

Ideally, pre-shift meetings should last ten or fifteen minutes. Any shorter and you don't have enough time to get anything done; any longer and you may start to lose the crew's attention.

I suggest you pick a specific meeting length and stick with it. I also encourage you to commit to starting and ending your meetings precisely on time – it will show that you take them seriously.

The internal element
The factor that most determines whether or not a staff meeting will be effective is the thinking of the manager or supervisor conducting it.

Do you approach your job like a cop, trying to find and correct mistakes or do you define your job as a coach, identifying and building on inherent strengths?

Do you see your staff as bunch of goof-offs looking for a free ride or as a group of intelligent adults who want to do the best job they can?

Do you think that management has to have all the answers or do you view your role as helping your crew discover the answers for themselves?

What you see is what you get.

Understanding comes from the inside out rather than from the outside in. When you have your own head in the right place, you can finally start to conduct staff meetings that will build confidence and involvement in your staff.

49
Step by step

Now that you understand that it is possible to hold energizing staff meetings, you may be anxious to get started. To help you get rolling, here is a suggested format for a 10-15 minute pre-shift meeting:

Good News (1-2 minutes)

The purpose here is to recognize what is working and set a positive tone for the meeting. You can talk about progress made toward a particular goal, share a success story about one of the staff or read a complimentary letter from a patron. Everybody likes to hear good news and it will help establish a warm feeling for the rest of the session, particularly when delivered with a feeling of sincere gratitude.

News of the Day (2-3 minutes)

In this segment you might talk briefly about what is coming up on this shift. Mention special promotions in effect and outline anything out of the ordinary that is happening. Be very focused and very brief. Don't get lost in this part of the program or you run the risk of sermonizing and killing the mood.

Staff Comments (5 minutes)

This is when you open the floor to the crew. It is the most important part of the meeting because it is when you can really find out what is happening and what is on people's minds. The critical skill is to listen without judging the comments you receive.

Avoid preconceived notions about what people might

be saying and be cautious about injecting your own thoughts into the discussion. This may take some practice but the results will be worth the effort.

Your goal is to create a safe environment for people to share their ideas and to learn from each other. This is where that all-important dialogue we discussed earlier really starts.

The quality and quantity of the input you receive will be in direct proportion to how well your staff feels you are listening to what they say – not just *hearing* the words, but really understanding the message.

Your willingness to consider their ideas will build trust and you will get more and more involvement from your crew as the level of trust in the organization improves.

At first, you may find that people are reluctant to open up. If your initial efforts to get people talking are greeted with silence, here are a few questions that may prompt some discussion:

Who deserves to be thanked or recognized and for what? What is making your job tough? What have you noticed that is improving? What are we doing that we should not be doing? What *aren't* we doing that we *should* be doing? Where is the system breaking down? What questions came up on your last shift that you couldn't answer? If this were your company, what would you change about it? You get the idea.

154

As people are talking, give them your undistracted attention. Listen to the feeling behind their words. You may want to ask if other people see things the same way as the speaker. You may want to ask a clarifying question to be sure you understand but resist the urge to add too many of your own comments.

New Information/Training (3-5 minutes)

Every gathering is an opportunity to enhance skills. Particularly in the beginning, shorten the time allocated to training by the time that the staff comments segment runs long. It is more important that you learn from the crew than that they learn from you.

Once they have confidence that there is a forum where their ideas will be heard and considered, your staff will be ready to receive new information. Use this part of the meeting to discuss a single point you want the staff to focus on for that shift, to impart product knowledge, to share professional tips or to amplify or supplement material from your regular training program.

Again, your own focus is important. Cut to the chase and don't ramble. People will be watching the time and you build credibility by being direct and finishing on schedule.

Effective staff meetings *are* possible. As your skills and credibility improve, you will see that staff meetings can be an easy way to begin creating a feeling of teamwork in your organization.

The exciting part is that they will also let you tap the inherent talents of your staff which will, in turn, help the manager's role evolve into one that is more enjoyable and less stressful.

50

Monitor your meetings

Now you have some ideas about staff meetings, but what about management gatherings? Are they any different? The short answer is that the dynamics are the same but since the format is usually different, it might help to apply the principles we have discussed to the typical management meeting.

While facilitating a management retreat for a major resort company, it became apparent that they had become addicted to griping. Their meetings typically turned into "bitch sessions" (and not surprisingly, everyone complained about that fact, too!)

Perhaps you have experienced this phenomenon in your own organization – it is not uncommon. But if this is not anyone's idea of a good time, why does it happen? More important, what can you do about it?

It starts with thinking
Earlier we discussed two modes of thinking – busy-minded thinking that is based on what you have in your memory and quiet-minded thinking that comes from tapping into a deeper flow of wisdom.

When people get caught in their own thoughts, the world takes on familiar patterns. The more deeply someone gets caught in their own thinking, the more convinced they are that their view of the world is "right" and any contradictory idea is "wrong."

On the other hand, quiet-minded thinking is the realm of insight and possibility. When the mind is quiet, people are not attached to their own thoughts and, instead, they easily entertain – even relish – the notions of others.

When the mind is quiet, you still have access to anything in your memory that is relevant, but you do not go into a situation preoccupied with old ideas.

We usually think of these shifts in our level of thinking as moods. More accurately, they are just a reflection of the extent to which you are attached to your own thoughts at a given moment.

Meetings have moods, too
Like people, meetings have moods – there are differing "tones" or feelings in the group which reflect the level of thinking of the participants. When the tone is high – when the participants' minds are quiet – everybody feels good together. Ideas flow easily, debate is spirited but respectful and the participants feel energized.

When a group is functioning at a high level, time flies. People in the group feel like they are learning new things – in fact they eagerly look for and explore ideas that differ from their own. They ask more questions and reflect more on the responses. These are the meetings that people look forward to attending.

As the tone deteriorates – as the participants become more attached to their own thinking – ideas start to become more tightly held. Dissenting opinions begin

157

to look like personal attacks and the participants increasingly feel drained.

The worse it gets, the worse it gets

As a group starts to slide down this slippery slope, agreement becomes more and more difficult. (As a parallel example, what are the odds that you will be able to successfully resolve anything with your mate when both of you are angry?)

The quality of conversation changes. Attitudes of "right" and "wrong" start to appear and the meeting can quickly reach a point where any sort of resolution or agreement is impossible.

If you described the levels of group functioning from higher to lower, it might look like this:

- Feeling like we all see eye to eye . . . and beyond!
- Feeling like we are really working together
- Feeling like we are committed to seeing each other's ideas clearly
- Feeling like it is getting hard to get our own ideas across to others
- Feeling bad enough to stop

Can you see these differences in your own experience of different meetings? If so, you are on your way to being able to do something about it. I will develop this idea more in a future book, but for now, just recognize and respect the importance of the tone in assuring productivity. Then monitor the tone of your meetings and notice when the feeling and the quality of the conversation starts to change.

The reasons aren't important

It doesn't matter why or what starts the group slipping into a lower tone, just start to be aware when it happens. Recognize and respect the symptoms for what they are – warning signs, not problems – and use this awareness to help your meetings become more enjoyable.

If you start to notice that the quality of discussion has taken a downward turn, resist the urge to make any group member wrong for being difficult. I hope by now you can see that assigning blame will only make things worse. If the group gets a little off track, just acknowledge the fact and call a recess. Sometimes a short break can help people reset.

If the group cannot get back in touch with that good feeling, call the meeting off and get together again later. Members of a truly healthy organization might agree as a group that they will discontinue a session if they start to function below a predetermined level.

Management meetings will become easier and more productive as the members of the group deepen their understanding of the relationship between thinking and behavior . . . and as their tolerance for conflict and ill will goes down.

51
Breaking old habits

Now that you have a different sense of your role as a manager and some ideas of how to achieve more with less effort, all you need to do to get your life back is to actually reduce the hours you spend on the job!

Long work schedules are just bad habits. I know how easy it is to get caught in the routine of endless hours but don't confuse activity with results – more hours do not necessarily equate to more results.

Less is more
Even the most dedicated manager starts wearing down – mentally if not physically – after 45 hours. As you get tired, you contribute to a lower work climate which costs the company money in terms of reduced productivity and irritated customers. On the other hand, when you come to the job enthusiastic and relaxed, you promote a more positive work climate.

(It is embarrassing to admit, but during that phase of my career when I worked 120-hour weeks, I knew that I was not getting the results. I also figured nobody would fire me if I was putting in that many hours!)

A few years ago, I created a formula for management compensation that called for paying a manager full wages . . . up to 45 hours a week. After that, it would take money away! Think of it as a four-step program for recovering workaholics!

I acknowledge there are busy periods in any business that require more hours on everyone's part (big sales, holidays and the like) and the formula is not intended to penalize anyone for being there during peak times. Still, there is a difference between long hours a week before Christmas and the same schedule during a routine week in mid-March.

Although I originally put this together in jest, I think it has value in forcing you to let go of routine tasks so you can free up enough time to actually have a life!

If you are presently working 60-70 hours a week, it is unrealistic to think you can cut your week back to 45 hours overnight. But you have to start somewhere and often it helps to have a little structure when changing old habits. Here's the way it works:

The formula
There are four levels in the formula, each calling for increased monetary penalties as the number of hours worked increases. This allows you to phase in the structure over time. For example, you might give managers 90 days to redistribute workloads before you implement Level 1. Three months later, Level 2 can kick in with Level 3 to follow 90 days later. Allow another three months before implementing Level 4 and you will have gradually nudged yourself (and your managers) into a liveable work week in only a year.

(If you choose to use this idea, discuss it with your managers first. Make sure everyone understands that the purpose of this structure is to help them get their lives back, not to punish them for working.)

MANAGEMENT COMPENSATION FORMULA

HOURS WORKED	LEVEL 1 %of Salary	LEVEL 2 %of Salary	LEVEL 3 %of Salary	LEVEL 4 %of Salary
45	100.0	100.0	100.0	100.0
46	100.0	99.5	99.0	98.5
47	100.0	99.0	98.0	97.0
48	100.0	98.5	97.0	95.5
45	100.0	98.0	96.0	94.0
50	100.0	97.5	95.0	92.5
51	99.5	96.5	93.5	90.5
52	99.0	95.5	92.0	88.5
53	98.5	94.5	90.5	86.5
54	98.0	93.5	89.0	84.5
55	97.5	92.5	87.5	82.5
56	96.5	91.0	85.5	80.0
57	95.5	89.5	83.5	77.5
58	94.5	88.0	81.5	75.0
59	93.5	86.5	79.5	72.5
60	92.5	85.0	77.5	70.0
61	91.0	83.0	75.0	67.0
62	89.5	81.0	72.5	64.0
63	88.0	79.0	70.0	61.0
64	86.5	77.0	67.5	58.0
65	85.0	75.0	65.0	55.0
66	83.0	72.5	62.0	51.5
67	81.0	70.0	59.0	48.0
68	79.0	67.5	56.0	44.5
69	77.0	65.0	53.0	41.0
70	75.0	62.5	50.0	37.5

If a manager can't produce the results you need in an average of 45 hours a week, you don't need him!

52
Closing comments

The ideas in this book may well have raised as many questions as they have answered . . . and what I have presented is, in fact, the tip of a much larger iceberg.

This is not information you **learn** as much as it is a set of principles you come to **understand** on deeper levels over time. Even as little as I understood when I arrived at the Olympic Training Center nearly 15 years ago was still enough to make an incredible difference in my effectiveness as a manager.

I saw results in six months that I would have been thrilled to accomplish in six years by any standard I ever had! I suspect that because my understanding of these principles has deepened since then, were I back in the same situation again, I might be able to achieve those results even faster.

Be willing to let it be easy
When you respect the power of a quiet mind, when you are willing to know less and listen more, exciting possibilities and insights will appear. The next steps you need to take will become obvious to you. You will be amazed at how smoothly life, both professionally and personally, will start to unfold.

The hardest part is allowing it to be that easy! The little voice in your head that has been saying, "There HAS to be an easier way to do this". . . is right!

I will leave you with one of my favorite quotes from Richard Bach, taken from his book, **Illusions.**

A modern parable

Once there lived a village of creatures along the bottom of a great crystal river. The current of the river swept silently over them all – young and old, rich and poor, good and evil, the current going its own way, knowing only its own crystal self.

Each creature in its own manner clung tightly to the twigs and rocks of the river bottom, for clinging was their way of life and resisting the current what each had learned from birth.

But one creature said at last, "I am tired of clinging. Though I cannot see it with my eyes, I trust that the current knows where it is going. I shall let go and let it take me where it will. Clinging I shall surely die of boredom."

The other creatures laughed and said, "Fool! Let go and that current you worship will throw you tumbled and smashed across the rocks and you will die quicker than boredom!"

But the one heeded them not, and taking a breath did let go and at once was tumbled and smashed by the current across the rocks. Yet in time, as the creature refused to cling again, the current lifted him free from the bottom and he was bruised and hurt no more.

And the creatures downstream, to whom he was a stranger, cried, "See a miracle! A creature like ourselves, yet he flies! See the Messiah, come to save us all!"

And the one carried in the current said, "I am no more Messiah that you. The river delights to lift us free if only we dare let go. Our true work is this voyage, this adventure."

But they cried the more, "Savior!" all the while clinging to the rocks, and when they looked again he was gone and they were left alone making legends of a Savior.

Appendix

Bill Marvin

Bill Marvin works with companies that want to get more done with less effort and with managers who want to get their lives back! He founded Effortless, Inc., a management research/education company and Prototype Restaurants, a hospitality consulting group.

Bill started his working life at the age of 14, washing dishes (by hand!) in a small restaurant on Cape Cod and went on to earn a degree in Hotel Administration from Cornell University. A veteran of the hospitality industry, Bill has managed hotels, institutions and clubs and owned full service restaurants.

He has had the keys in his hand, his name on the loans and the payrolls to meet. His professional curiosity and practical experience enable him to grasp (and teach) the human factors common to the growth and success of every type of service-oriented enterprise.

He is a member of the Council of Hotel and Restaurant Trainers and the National Speakers Association. He has achieved all major professional certifications in the foodservice industry. He is a prolific author and writes regular columns in the trade magazines of several industries.

In addition to a limited private consulting practice, he logs over 150,000 miles annually delivering corporate keynote addresses and conducting staff and management training programs in the US, Canada, Europe and the Pacific Rim.

For more information, contact Bill Marvin at:

EFFORTLESS, INC.
PO Box 280 · Gig Harbor, WA 98335-0280 USA

Voice: (253) 858-9255 or (800) 767-1055
Fax: (253) 851-6887 or (888) 767-1055
e-mail: bill@restaurantdoctor.com
Internet website: www.restaurantdoctor.com

167

Reading and Resources

Here is a current summary of materials and services available from Bill Marvin and Effortless, Inc.

Books and Materials

Restaurant Basics: Why Guests Don't Come Back and What You Can Do About It, 1992, John Wiley & Sons

The Foolproof Foodservice Selection System: The Complete Manual for Creating a Quality Staff, 1993, John Wiley & Sons

From Turnover to Teamwork: How to Build and Retain a Customer-Oriented Foodservice Staff, 1994, John Wiley & Sons

50 Tips to Improve Your Tips: The Service Pro's Guide to Delighting Diners, 1995, Hospitality Masters Press

Guest-Based Marketing: How to Gain Foodservice Volume Without Losing Your Shirt, 1997, John Wiley & Sons

50 Proven Ways to Build Restaur59ant Sales & Profit, 1997, Hospitality Masters Press (editor and contributing author)

Cashing In On Complaints: Turning Disappointed Diners Into Gold, 1997, Hospitality Masters Press

50 Proven Ways to Enhance Guest Service, 1998, Hospitality Masters Press (editor and contributing author)

50 Proven Ways to Build More Profitable Menus, 1998, Hospitality Masters Press (editor and contributing author)

50 Money-Making Marketing Ideas: Increasing Sales by Improving Repeat Patronage, 1999, Hospitality Masters Press

More Restaurant Basics: Why Guests Don't Come Back and What You Can Do About It, 1999, Hospitality Masters Press

Bill also offers audio and video training programs, manuals and computer text files . . . and the list grows steadily. For a current catalog and price list, phone (800) 767-1055 or fax your request toll-free to (888) 767-1055. Locally or outside the US and Canada, call (253) 858-9255 or fax (253) 851-6887.

Keynotes and Seminars

Bill Marvin is generally regarded as the most-booked speaker in the hospitality industry and his messages apply equally well to any service-oriented business. No other speaker takes a similar approach to his subjects, especially in the areas of human relations and organizational effectiveness. He is also one of the few conducting training seminars for the hourly staff.

His keynotes and seminars focus on the human dimensions of hospitality, customer service, staff selection and retention. He is also in demand as a facilitator for executive retreats. When it comes to dealing with people or managing an organization, if you have ever thought, "There *has* to be an easier way to do this," schedule a house call from the Restaurant Doctor™ (even if you are not in the hospitality business!)

Consulting Services

Bill's active speaking schedule does not leave much time for private consulting, but he is always open to an interesting offer and accepts one or two projects a year to keep his skills sharp. His expertise is in the areas of concept development/refinement and increasing sales, retention and productivity by enhancing the work climate of the company.

He has recently started one-on-one coaching with executives who want to deepen their understanding of the principles presented in this book to improve their professional effectiveness . . . and get their lives back!

Newsletters

Bill produces "Electronic House Call," a free weekly newsletter sent by e-mail. To be placed on the EHC mailing list, send your name and e-mail address to bill@restaurantdoctor.com.

Bill also produces a bimonthly "Home Remedies" newsletter. To receive a free six-month trial subscription, contact Bill by phone, fax or e-mail and ask for the application form.

169

Has this book got you thinking?

If you found the ideas in this book intriguing, you will want a copy of *The Effortless Organization* by Bill Marvin and Robert Kausen, scheduled for publication in the fall of 1999.

The Effortless Organization will explore in greater depth what has been presented in this book and offer examples of how these principles have been applied to a broad range of issues in a wide spectrum of industries. It will enhance your understanding of how to get more done with less effort . . . and have a life!

To obtain a copy for your library, contact Effortless, Inc., PO Box 280, Gig Harbor, WA 98335 or go to www.effortless-org.com for ordering information.